FROM JAY-Z TO JESUS

Reaching & Teaching Young Adults in the Black Church

BENJAMIN STEPHENS III / RALPH C. WATKINS

JUDSON PRESS

PUBLISHERS SINCE 1824

VALLEY FORGE, PA

FROM JAY-Z TO JESUS:
Reaching & Teaching Young Adults in the Black Church

Judson Press and the authors have made every effort to trace the ownership of all quotes. In the event of a question arising from the use of a quote, we regret any error made and will be pleased to make the necessary correction in future printings and editions of this book.

Unless otherwise indicated, Bible quotations are taken from the New King James Version. Copyright © 1982 by Thomas Nelson, Inc. Used by permission. All rights reserved.

Bible quotations marked NIV are taken from the HOLY BIBLE, NEW INTER-NATIONAL VERSION®. NIV®. Copyright © 1973, 1978, 1984 by International Bible Society. Used by permission of Zondervan. All rights reserved.

Library of Congress Cataloging-in-Publication Data
Stephens, Benjamin.
From Jay-Z to Jesus: reaching & teaching young adults in the Black church/
Benjamin Stephens III, Ralph C. Watkins.—1st ed.
p. cm.
ISBN 978-0-8170-1545-9 (pbk. : alk. paper) 1. African American young adults—Religious life. 2. Church work with young adults. I. Watkins, Ralph C. II. Title.
BV4468.2.A34S74 2009
259'.2508996073—dc22
                                                                          2008049473
Printed in the U.S.A.
First Edition, 2009.

To the women who have always
believed in the God
in me and pushed me to pursue my dreams:
my mother, Earlene Watkins,
my sister, Cynthia Washington,
and my wife, Vanessa Watkins.
—Ralph C. Watkins

To my Lord and Savior, Jesus Christ—
he is truly the best thing that
has ever happened to me.

To my late grandmothers, Gladys R. Yancy
and Joyce Neal—your legacy is with me always,
now and for eternity.

To the greatest parents on earth,
Benjamin Jr. and Rita Stephens.

And to my inspiration,
the woman of my dreams
and love of my life,
Lady Latonya Stephens.

I love you all and could not have
made it without you.
—Ben Stephens

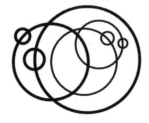

FOREWORD

The black church has been the most enduring organic institution created by Africans on the soil of North America. The church has nurtured our freedom movements and been the birthplace of our greatest cultural creations: the spirituals, jazz, the blues, gospel, R&B, and neo-soul. All have a connection to the faith community we call the church. The one cultural creation not tied *directly* to the church is the newest child in African American culture: hip hop.

The church has had a difficult time coming to grips with the unique urban phenomenon called hip hop. The responses range from vitriolic damnation to an uneasy embrace of a culture few within the sheltered community of the church understand. In his first book, *The Gospel Remix: Reaching the Hip Hop Generation,* Dr. Ralph Watkins became one of the few scholars and ministers who have taken up the task of reaching out to the generation caught in the gap between the "mic" and the minister. His thoughtful analysis and loving critiques have raised profound questions for clergy and scholars alike. How do we engage the generations raised in a multimedia, post-Christian, and postmodern context? How will the church effectively evangelize a community influenced by the market and media? Can the black church regain her relevancy among the young adults challenged and spiritually hungry generation?

In this second book, Dr. Watkins and his coauthor, Rev. Benjamin Stephens, look beyond the maturing hip hop generation to the generation that follows—today's young adults (ages

18–39) who have been raised in the culture of hip hop and who have more challenging questions and more complex concepts of spirit-uality than any previous generation in recent memory. In *From Jay-Z to Jesus,* Dr. Watkins and Rev. Stephens offer church leaders insights and guidelines for developing a relevant and inviting ministry that will reintroduce this generation, who already know Jay-Z intimately, to a different and better role model, Jesus Christ. These pages will compel even the most conservative and old-school reader to reflect inwardly and to rethink existing assumptions about how ministry in the black church ought to be done.

I first met Dr. Watkins in Augusta, Georgia, where he was serving as associate pastor of the Beulah Grove Baptist Church and teaching sociology at Augusta State University. Students clamored to get into his classes to learn from the minister, DJ, and scholar. He brought local clergy into the academy and challenged them to rethink evangelism, theology, and archaic doctrines of "what is appropriate" in the twenty-first century in order to reach this generation. Through teaching, pastoral ministry, and personal mentoring, Ralph has ushered a host of young adults into a radical and redemptive relationship with Jesus. You'll hear some of their stories in this book, and you'll glimpse the legacy that has made it a delight for me to be associated with Dr. Watkins, whom I consider a friend and colleague. His exemplary work and loving critique has enriched my life, and I know this book will be a blessing to your personal library and Christian ministry. It is my prayer that this practical volume will enable you to find new ways to connect with the doo-wop, bebop, and hip-hop generations.

—Otis Moss III
Senior Pastor
Trinity United Church Of Christ

INTRODUCTION

"Go therefore and make disciples of all the
nations, baptizing them in the name of the Father
and of the Son and of the Holy Spirit, teaching
them to observe all things that I have commanded you; and lo, I am with you always, even to the
end of the age." Amen.
MATTHEW 28:19-20

Young adult ministry in the African American church is not a new
idea. Rev. Walter Arthur McCray wrote a book in 1986 titled
Black Young Adults: How to Reach Them, What to Teach Them.
The cover copy included this description: "Strengthening the
Black Church and Community by Educating Black Young Adults
Ages 17–24."[1] McCray understood that serving young adults
would strengthen both them as a group and the community as a
whole. He and his peers saw the need for and importance of
young adult ministry in the African American church more than
twenty years ago, and they took action. I am a product of that era
and that ministry. The African American churches that met the
special needs of young adults are now benefiting from that work
in that they have a solid base of mature adults who are serving
as the foundation of their congregations. On the other hand,
churches who missed this call have aging congregations absent of
young adults. This book is a word of hope and a biblically based
action plan to help those churches reach young adults and develop them in the faith of Jesus Christ.

The church needs young adults, and young adults need the church. The authors of the book *The Quest for Christ: Discipling Today's Young Adults,* Ken Baugh and Rich Hurst contend:

> While our churches should be full of young adults...it is the unfortunate fact that churches are devoid of them because [young adults] don't come to church. Church doesn't make sense to many young adults; it doesn't address things important to them. So what? Why should we care? Why can't young adults just get with the program and fit into our way of doing things? Why do we have to cater to their whims? The answer is obvious of course. The Great Commission tells us to "go and make disciples."[2]

Baugh and Hurst make reaching young adults a commission issue, and that is just what it is. God is calling the church to respond as Jesus commanded us to go and make disciples out of a generation that is lost and trying to find its way. The young adults in the African American community are lost in a post-soul, post–civil rights era, and they are looking for direction. While popular culture is sending them all kinds of mixed messages, they need a word from God. This book is meant to help every congregation, small or large, to respond to this call.

This book is an answer to this commission while simultaneously being a call to reach young adults with the gospel. We use the ages eighteen to thirty-nine as our target group, because young adulthood has been prolonged. In the good old days people went to college from ages eighteen to twenty-two, got a job, got married, bought a house, and the rest was history. Today young adults are staying home longer, taking on average five to six years to finish college, and delaying marriage. As a result, we have prolonged adolescence and prolonged young adult status. As young adults mature, the process extends well into their thirties. We will help readers understand the transitions young adults are going through and provide a biblically based model to help young adults become what God has designed them to become.

Every congregation should be fully submitted to their pastor while being led by the Holy Spirit as to how they should respond to this call. We trust you will be inspired as God leads you and your church to meet the needs of God's precious young adults.

NOTES

1. Walter Arthur McCray, *Black Young Adults: How to Reach Them, What to Teach Them* (Chicago: Black Light Fellowship, 1986).

2. Ken Baugh and Rich Hurst, *The Quest for Christ: Discipling Today's Young Adults* (Loveland, CO: Group, 2003), 9.

1

Why Do We Need a Young Adult Ministry?

> Therefore I remind you to stir up the gift of God
> which is in you through the laying on of my
> hands. For God has not given us a spirit of fear,
> but of power and of love and of a sound mind.
>   2 TIMOTHY 1:6-7

We open with this word of encouragement from the apostle Paul to his young colleague in ministry, Timothy, as he is being called to lead. As Timothy steps up to the plate, he is questioning his fitness for ministry and may be a bit intimidated, but Paul reminds him of who he is in God. Paul reminds him that he is gifted and that God has given him a spirit of power, love, and a sound mind. To put it in Ebonics, Paul is saying, "Don't be trippin' you got this. You have been called, so go and do you. Do you as God has called you to be you."

This conversation between Paul and Timothy is the epitome of young adult ministry. While young adults are trying to define who they are and what they are called to do, they are second-guessing themselves, their God, and their faith. Young adults are caught in an intense period of transition. Just as adults go through a midlife

1

crisis in their late forties or early fifties, young adults have a quarter-life crisis sometime between their late teens and late twenties. Young adults need to have peers and elders with whom they can have the type of conversation that Paul and Timothy were having. They need a place to ask questions, express doubts and fears, and deal with the wonderment as they close the first quarter of their lives. The fact that the Timothys and Tammys of the world need to have such conversations is reason enough to have a young adult ministry. But if you aren't convinced yet, keep walking with us. We will share with you our experience as ministers to young adults, include what the research has shown, and weave in the testimonials of young adults.

Who Are Young Adults?

Young adults—those from ages eighteen to thirty-nine—face unique challenges based on their age and stage in life that require special attention. Therefore they can't be lumped into the general congregation as simply "adults." This is especially true for African American young adults living in a post-civil rights, post-soul generation that is seeking direction about what it means to be a Christian and an African American in this day.

The struggle of young adult African Americans to achieve success takes place against a backdrop of isolated examples of successful African Americans—some who are much older—and they are asked, "Why can't you do what I did?" Working-class African Americans have come under attack from both within and outside the community; this is especially true of the working poor.[1] God forbid they actually love hip-hop culture and music; how does the church integrate this dichotomy? African American young adults are condemned for their culture and music both on the news and in the church. They feel locked in and locked out. How does the church minister to this unique subset of people who need the church? They are begging the church to hear their cries and respond.

Success in their struggles for relationships with their elders, with God, and with the larger African American community is what young adults need. How is that relationship facilitated? Who is going to make the invitation for them to come to the table? Who is going to set the table for the conversation? In the passage that opened this chapter, we see that Paul set the table and invited Timothy. Paul's relationship with Timothy is a model of how to mentor young adults, to allow them to walk with you as you walk with them, lead with them, and turn over leadership to them.

One criticism young adults have of their elders is that the elders have held on too long. The elders' refusal to hand the wheel to the next generation has displaced young adults within the African American community and left a void in the leadership ranks. It is the young who have radical approaches and tend to lead progressive movements for change. When you check the resumes of the majority of the major civil rights leaders from the 1960s, they were young adults when they hit the streets and called for change. They had mentors; their elders empowered them by developing them and encouraging them to lead. If the agenda for change and leadership in the African American community is to reemerge, it will be with our young adults. But for this to happen, the church has to help them walk through this period in their lives.

What Help Do Young Adults Need?

Young adults need help answering the questions life is throwing at them in their transition years, and the church is the place where dialogue around these issues should occur. This dialogue and development are best facilitated in a young adult ministry that focuses on and responds to the specific needs and concerns of young adults. Young adults come to church with head and heart;

they are thinkers who are trying to deal with their feelings. This crowd walks into the church with suspicion, so young adult ministry must respond to them with intentionality. They come to church to ask probing questions, and in many cases the church setting isn't prepared to handle what young adults bring to the table. A brief story out of Ralph's experience illustrates this point.

Why Do We Need a Young Adult Ministry? A True Story

It was a Tuesday evening in October 2006—a normal Tuesday night Bible study session at First African Methodist Episcopal Church in Los Angeles (FAME). Our pastor, Dr. John Hunter, came in after the devotion period and did a wonderful job teaching. What stood out about the night's class was that actress and singer Brandy and a few of her friends were in attendance. I noticed them right away. They were sitting at the table in front of my wife and me. I was taken by Brandy's presence because my daughters loved her. She was the star of the television show *Moesha*, and she had a successful singing career in the late 1990s. I was excited to see her. I whispered to my wife, "That's Brandy." During the study all went well. At the outset of the study, one of the guests with Brandy asked Pastor John if there was going to be a time for questions. Pastor John responded in his normal kind and compassionate voice that there would be a time for questions at the end of the study.

When the time for questions came, the atmosphere in the room took a turn. The young man who had asked about questions earlier got up and asked one question and then proceeded to ask a series of questions. He then requested the microphone, and his questioning became almost hostile. Pastor John attempted to answer what he could discern as questions. The young brother was persistent, and I could sense that the issues he was raising weren't going to be answered in one night's session. He needed a relationship in the context of ministry that would facilitate an ongoing dialogue. Others in the study jumped in lovingly, offering support in answering the young man's queries. Then Brandy raised a question in regard to lust and sin. I offered an answer and directed her to James 1:13–15. My answer didn't appear to suffice, so one of my colleagues in the ministry who was sitting closer to Brandy than I began to talk with her.

Brandy switched seats and settled next to my colleague in ministry. She shared with Brandy more specifically, and the discussion appeared to be productive. As the question and answer period drew to a close, one could sense the tension in the room. Some of the elder church members were visibly aggravated by the line and tone of the questioning. I was not bothered at all, for after working with young adults all of my adult life, I knew this was how young adults sought answers. I was invigorated. At the end of the study, we circled for our normal prayer; the praise leader of the study played a closing song and praise danced in the middle of the prayer circle, which is normal for him. Brandy joined him, and all was well.

But as the prayer concluded, one of the regular attendees of FAME got verbally loud with a member of Brandy's crew. He was upset by the line of questions that had been raised. The young man in Brandy's crew didn't respond and appeared to be taken aback by the verbal jarring. The conversation between the two men got louder, and others looked on as a crowd circled around them as if a fight were going on. The tension spiraled. Finally, the exchange ended, but we would later find out that it wasn't done at all.

The next week FAME church was on national radio. The *Tom Joyner Morning Show* did a piece on the incident, and I had to respond on behalf of the church on the show the next week. Then the November 20, 2006, issue of the *National Enquirer* ran the story "A True Bible Thumping: Singer Brandy & Pals in Big

Brawl at Church." What? This was unbelievable. Our church was in the *National Enquirer*! Before and after the story broke, Pastor John talked about the Bible study episode, and the sentiment at that time was sorrowful. It was a shame that the incident had escalated to this point.

Pastor John talked about the need for a young adult Bible study that was dialogical, that centered around asking and answering questions. I felt that I had to examine what had happened and what God was saying to us. When I looked back at that evening, I remembered that as the intense questioning period began a sister came up to me and whispered in my ear, "See, we really do need that young adult Bible study now." I responded with a cursory nod, but as this event escalated, it became the alarm calling me to young adult ministry. If I had been unclear about the need for young adult ministry in my new church, it was clear now.

Lessons Learned

The lesson made clear at FAME was that young adults need a place to raise questions. They need a place to negotiate their journey in a faith community that isn't judging them or pushing them but is instead lovingly walking beside them as they find their way, being led by the Holy Spirit. Such a ministry calls for dialogue that intentionally and directly engages the world young adults live in on a daily basis while helping them through the maturation process.

Young adults are trying to live edited lives in an unedited world. They are asking questions about identity, purpose, and meaning making—questions rooted in their faith quest. Sharon Parks, who has done groundbreaking research on young adults, defines the young adult years as a time of faith formation, loss, and recovery of faith. Parks says, "Typically, in the years from seventeen to thirty a distinctive mode of meaning-making can emerge....This mode of making meaning includes (1) becoming critically aware of one's own composing of reality, (2) self-consciously participating in an ongoing dialogue toward truth, (3) cultivating a capacity to respond—to act—in ways that are satisfying and just."[2]

Young adults are trying to make sense in and out of a world that is overloading them with mixed messages. They are asking questions such as the following:

What is faith?
What is religion?
How am I in the world and not of the world?
How do I live my faith?
How much of my parents' religion do I want or
    don't want?
Do I need the church to live a spiritual life?
What kind of church—if any—should I go to?

Many young adults are asking and dealing with these questions outside the sacred walls of the church. Research by the Barna Group offers six findings that confirm that although young adults have spiritual and religious urges, they aren't attending church on a regular basis.

1. Millions of twentysomething Americans—many of whom were active in churches during their teens—pass through their most formative adult decade while putting Christianity on the back burner.

2. Only three out of ten twentysomethings (31%) attend church in a typical week. Conversely, close to 70 percent don't attend church.

3. The research shows that church attendance bottoms out during the late twenties when the vast majority of

students have transitioned from education to the workforce. Just 22 percent of those ages twenty-five to twenty-nine attended church in the last week.

4. Many twentysomethings are reversing course after having been active church attenders during their teenage years. As teenagers, more than half attended church each week. From high school graduation to age twenty-five there is a 42 percent drop in weekly church attendance and a 58 percent decline from age eighteen to age twenty-nine.

5. More than eight out of ten twentysomethings (80%) said that their religious faith is very important in their life, and nearly six out of ten (57%) claimed to have made a personal commitment to Jesus Christ that is still important in their lives.

6. The study also showed that young adults are only slightly less likely than older adults to pray, which reflects their appetite for personal spiritual experience. Three-quarters of young adults in their twenties (75%) said they had prayed to God in the past week.[3]

Young adults are praying and seeking God but not with the support of a church family. They need a young adult ministry that will welcome them, walk with them on their journeys, and provide them with relevant worship experiences. Churches that are intentional in developing young adult ministry will see an influx of young adults seeking an informed faith that speaks to both head and heart. Young adults want to be able to ask questions without rebuke but with a loving, informed answer that engages sacred text while respecting their personal journeys.

Sensitivity to their journeys must be demonstrated in tangible, observable acts that young adults can relate to. They don't want to be set aside and treated like they are the church of tomorrow; they want to be active in the life of the church today. Yes, they are the church's future, and the church that fails to develop its young adults is a church that will not have a future. Therefore active care for and involvement of young adults must begin now. This ministry is important to the very life and future of the African American church.

The questions young adults have are too big and too critical to push aside. When I have this conversation with some of my friends who are senior pastors, they talk about the way it used to be when we were coming through. When we were in our twenties and thirties, churches had no young adult ministries; we just made it through. So why do we need young adult ministries today? Because we are dealing with a generation of African Americans who haven't grown up in the church, and they aren't coming to church now. We have a few exceptions, but as a rule young adults are absent from our churches. We need them, and they need us.

The model of old has become obsolete. It served us well, but it is outmoded today. I have an old record player in my living room that I refuse to throw away. It can't play CDs or MP3 files, so I also have a CD player and an iPod. Likewise, some once useful ministry methods no longer work with modern young adults and need to be replaced by new ones. Specialized ministries to segments of the church are necessary.

Lost in Church: "Where Do I Fit?"
A Young Single Mother Tells Her Story
by Jeneen L. Robinson

Jeneen is an associate minister at Bethel African Methodist Episcopal Church in Los Angeles. She is a thirty-two-year-old single mother and a graduate of Fuller Theological Seminary. She is also an actress and was featured in the PBS documentary The Call *in 2008.*

I once left a church because it focused on marriage and family too much. I'm not married and at that time didn't have a family of my own; I did not fit in. Why should I sit through sermon after sermon about how God can make your marriage work when I am not married? What I really want is a better job and to buy a house! I just did not fit in. Once I had my first child, I was tempted to leave church again, because as a single parent, I did not fit in. After all, the perfect Christian family consists of a husband, a wife, 2.5 kids, and a dog, right? Negative. Most of the sisters I know raising kids alone didn't dare go to church for fear of being looked at, not as *sister girl*, but as *sinner girl*. The ministry of the church today fails to acknowledge and minister to blended families; it still upholds the view of the perfect Christian family that is no longer a reality for many.

When my son was still a baby, I always sat in the back and on an aisle seat just in case we had to make a run for the restroom. And let's not forget to mention the "cry room," where mothers sat in exile with their fretful offspring. Once there, there were so many babies crying, I still could not hear the sermon. Going to church on Sunday seemed useless. Trying to remain hopeful and optimistic, I tried weekday services and church outreach opportunities. Um, let's look at the bulletin:

> **Bible Study, 7:00 p.m.:** "Too late, too dark, too cold. Can't drag my child out this late; it's his bedtime!"
> Three-day Weekend Marriage Retreat (couples only): "That's easy—I'm not married."
> **Prison Ministry:** "Not in prison, at least not that kind of prison."
> **Women's Prayer Breakfast:** "Why do people in church always eat when praying? In the Bible, prayer is always associated with fasting, not eating. Why don't we exercise faith and work out?"
> **Youth Lock-In:** "Not that young and don't wanna chaperone."

Men's Golfing Ministry: "Yeah, right."
Singles Outing: "But who's gonna watch the baby?"

Have you ever looked at the bulletin and nothing fit? What is supposed to radiate inclusion to you instead reeks of exclusion. What is there in the black church for young adult women, particularly single mothers, to do? When do we get ministered to? If they're like me, young adult women are screaming and no one is listening. *Help!*

Young adult women have other reasons for not attending church. Many are excuses I have used. We are tired of getting "picked on" by the church mothers because of how we dress and how we look. Don't hate us 'cause we're beautiful! Who said that once you're saved you have to walk around in sackcloth and ashes? I still want to look good. Then they bring you the unwanted lap scarf to cover your kneecaps. If my kneecaps will send someone to hell, then he really doesn't know Jesus in the first place. Get a life, church mother! Ain't nobody worried about my kneecaps but you.

Mother's Day is the worst for single mothers. It is on that day that we get the fake Christian smile and pity party applause and the words "Hang in there" or "We love you." Then the flowers go to the oldest mother of the church and the youngest mother. But every other day of the year single mothers get badgered by the church for having had children out of wedlock (as if they did it alone). They get blamed for the fathers not being in their children's lives (they must be angry black women). And then we have to deal with the women who fear that we may be after their husbands. Gimme a break! Didn't I get enough of your crucifying me when you didn't come to my baby shower because you think single mothers don't deserve one?

Titus 2:3 says that older women in the church should be reverent, not slanderers. They should not talk about how single moms can't cook, can't keep it together, and don't know how to raise a child 'cause we're just children ourselves. Stop prejudging and thinking that we always need to be told what to do and how to do it. We need to start with respect—mutual respect for who we are in Christ. Then real ministry will begin when women unveil themselves. If the older women will begin to unveil what they went through and how they got through it that would be true ministry to young adult women. That would be nourishing to my soul.

I eventually found my place in church—God called me to ministry. But honestly, had I not been called, I would have left church for good. I have an opportunity now to help young women find a place in church. Will you?

QUESTIONS TO CONSIDER

1. Where is the place for young adults in your church? If your answer is "everywhere," then it's nowhere. When my kids were little, they had full run of the house, but they still had their own room. Where is the place for young adults in your church?

2. How does your church make a place for young adults?

3. What are the obstacles to young adult ministry?

4. Does your church have a place and a time led by someone who loves young adults for young adults to ask questions?

5. Is there a congregational or at least a pastoral recognition of the struggles, challenges, and developmental transitions that young adults are going through?

NOTES

1. See Bill Cosby and Alvin F. Poussaint, *Come On, People: On the Path from Victims to Victors* (Nashville: Nelson, 2007); see also Michael E. Dyson, *Is Bill Cosby Right? Or Has the Black Middle Class Lost Its Mind?* (New York: Basic Civitas Books, 2005).

2. Sharon Daloz Parks, *Big Questions, Worthy Dreams: Mentoring Young Adults in Their Search for Meaning, Purpose, and Faith* (San Francisco: Jossey-Bass, 2000), 4.

3. "The Barna Report 2006." http://www.barna.org/FlexPage.aspx?Page=BarnaUpdate&BarnaUpdateID=149, accessed November 24, 2008.

2

Building on a Strong Foundation: A Biblical Foundation for Young Adult Ministry

> …we should no longer be children, tossed to and fro and carried about with every wind of doctrine, by trickery of men, in the cunning craftiness of deceitful plotting, but, speaking the truth in love…grow up in all things into Him who is the head—Christ.
> EPHESIANS 4:14-15

The need for young adult ministry is evidenced by the fact that young adults are not returning to church even while they are trying to figure out spiritual questions in the world. This signals a major problem that only the church can solve. Thus the young adult ministry needs a solid biblical and theological foundation that can stand the test of time. Without such a solid base, ministry leaders may be tempted to build a ministry that is "contemporary" or "faddish." But young adult ministry shouldn't be treated as a passing thing, for it is just as vital as the church's youth ministry. The heart of young adult ministry consists of forming ambassadors for Christ as young adults are trying to find their new selves in Christ in their evolution from adolescence to adulthood.

In this chapter we will see that Jesus was intimately involved in young adult ministry and that young adult ministry is biblically founded and supported. The church must establish a partnership with young adults in the empowerment process of developing a smart faith that helps them deal with the tensions inherent in living the Christian life. Such a partnership helps them engage the world from a biblical perspective that empowers them to lead a moral and ethical life that is informed by God's Word. This term "smart faith" was given to us by J. P. Moreland and Mark Matlock who say that "biblical faith is a power or skill to act in accordance with the nature of the kingdom of God and trust in what we have reason to believe is true. This is faith built on reason."[1]

If we are going to partner with our young adults on the journey they are taking, we are going to have to take their faith development seriously. One goal of our walking with them should be to help them love and know God with their entire person while discovering God's purpose for their lives. And we should also be striving to integrate them into the mainstream life of the church. When young adults are empowered with a smart faith, they learn to lovingly engage the world and those who have yet to accept the lifestyle of the Christian faith. This teaching should be done in concert with a living faith—a teaching in action that takes the faith into the world and helps them engage real-life situations and reflect on how their faith informs their actions and reactions. This teaching ministry that helps them apply their faith 24/7 in every situation is critical for young adults as they seek to live an integrated life of faith that is not simply reflected in a Sunday institutional worship service bogged down with ritual and irrelevance.

As we said earlier, young adults are seeking spiritual and religious answers in the world. This is especially true of unchurched young adults for whom popular culture is offering answers. This is a very religious generation, so the church must take note of how young adults access religious teaching so that it builds its young adult ministry in conversation with what they are getting outside the church. Robin Sylvan, in his book *Traces of the Spirit: The Religious Dimensions of Popular Music*, says that this generation is not less religious but rather is finding new ways, in the context of popular culture, to express and define their religious and spiritual life.[2] In an age where rappers are becoming spiritual leaders, young adults have big questions. They are being bombarded with what Sylvan calls "cultural religion."[3] This cultural religion is a religious ethos and belief system developed in and espoused by popular culture. It involves a remix or syncretism of religious systems and traditions. Five-percenter theology (which is a mix of Nation of Islam theology and black consciousness thinking)[4], Islam, and hip-hop are advancing as types of religion.

In the midst of divergent religious worldviews, young adults who consider themselves Christians are trying not to be judgmental and closed-minded while simultaneously trying to believe there is only one name by which people might be saved. They are sitting at the crossroads of faith not knowing how to engage in civil conversation about such important topics. They wonder how to negotiate this diverse religious terrain while both following and being critical of their parents' faith.

Young Adult Ministry: Jesus' Model of Engagement

As Jesus walked with his disciples, he talked about and dealt with the issues of the day. He directly taught about and modeled engagement with the world and confronted tradition and error. As Jesus challenged tradition and healed on the Sabbath, and as he dealt with accusations, he marked out a way to traverse competing traditions while modeling the right way in love. After

Jesus anointed the twelve disciples on the mountainside (Mark 3:13-19), he took them down the mountain for ministry in a world of competing religious ideals and traditions. They faced a host of critics who opposed them for doing good (3:20-30). The teachers of the law went so far as to say that Jesus received his power from demons. Jesus' response to this accusation provides an example of dialogue with his religious opponents both for the disciples and for young adults today. Jesus reasoned with them, asking questions that led to reasoned answers. He modeled a way to have a civil conversation about divisive issues of faith. For Jesus to do what he did in this example (3:20-30) and in other confrontations throughout Scripture, he had to know the tradition he was challenging. He lovingly and willing engaged those of that tradition and then offered a right alternative through a model of dialogue rooted in a reasoned faith that would help them see and accept the Truth.

The world of faith today is streaming from the Internet and revolving on compact discs. The religious pundits are not speaking from pulpits, but rather at concerts in between their songs. They are speaking on CDs as they outline their faith and their version of Christianity. As young adults sit with their friends and listen to the latest CD release or watch the latest video on Black Entertainment Television or Music Television, they need to be able to share their faith in an intelligent, effective manner. They need a smart faith that is in touch with the real world, one concerned with and knowledgeable about other traditions. Young adults not only need to be ready to give an answer for their hope (1 Peter 3:15), but they need to be giving hope in their answer. To respond to young adults with religious platitudes—"The Bible says it, I believe it, and that settles it"—will not work, and it is not helpful for them in the world they live in. In other words, 1 Peter 3:15-16 must be made flesh: "But in your hearts set apart Christ as Lord. Always be prepared to give an answer to everyone who asks you to give the reason for the hope that you have. But do this with gentleness and respect, keeping a clear conscience, so that those who speak maliciously against your good behavior in Christ may be ashamed of their slander" (1 Peter 3:15-16 NIV).

Young adults must be encouraged to learn about and fully engage the pluralistic religious world in which they live. Books and speakers on traditions contrary to Christianity must be a highlight of young adult religious training. The works of artists like KRS-One, Erykah Baydu, Jill Scott, Lauryn Hill, Talib Kweli, Mos Def, and others could be center stage in this conversation. Bible teaching that engages the world through dialogue won't retard, distort, or tear up the faith of young adults; it will build up their faith. It will give them the ability to engage the world with a faith of informed reason. We need to arm young adults with theological resources just as Jesus equipped his disciples, for the intent of young adult ministry is to make mature disciples of Jesus Christ. Bible teaching that models how to engage the real world with the Word empowers young adults. Such teaching will give them both a reason and a method to engage other traditions on solid ground. A faith without a rational, learned component will fail young adults in the pluralistic world in which they live.

What You Lookin' For?

In the context of a convoluted and pluralistic world, the bottom line is that young adults are searching for meaning. They are looking for something they can hold to, believe, and build a life with—not merely a foundation of religious tradition. In fact, religion as presented in some contexts is more a hindrance to real faith development than a help. Antagonism to the word *religion* is strong among young adults, so using *religion* and *faith* interchangeably causes problems. *Religion* is seen as something that is institutionalized and intolerant. *Faith* and meaning must be freed from the chains of religion and become something one can hold on to as a life guide based on a set of godly ethical and moral principles.

Jesus took his disciples on a spiritual quest for true faith in God that fueled how they lived for him in a community of believers and nonbelievers. Faith became a life-giving rather than a life-strangling affair. Sharon Parks, the author of the book *Big Questions*, puts it this way: "Faith is to point toward the meaning-making that frames, colors, provides tone and texture, and realizes the activity of everyday."[5] Faith is intentionally developed as it engages and helps makes sense of everyday life. It can handle complex relationships and tensions without giving simplistic, trite answers rooted in a limited exegesis of Scripture.

Young adults need a faith that helps make meaning and provides a foundation for those struggling to make sense of the world in which they are searching for their place. This faith must be strong enough to deal with the paradoxes of a just God who watches an unjust world. It must be a complex faith that deals with the grey areas. Such faith must give meaning that fills in the blanks, while at the same time allow for some blanks to be left unfilled—teaching how one can walk without having all the answers. This faith quest must be spiritual enough and supportive enough to offer a place of comfort, yet also keep ethical challenges as one of the central theological and practical tenets of young adult ministry.[6] Young adult ministries must form communities that provide comfort among peers and a space where they are challenged to align what they say they believe with living lives that affirm those beliefs.

Where Are We Going?

Young adults are in a world they know needs changing, and they are the ones to lead change. They are open to change because where they are in life is a time of intense change. The question is how the church will help facilitate and empower them in these moments of change so that they can feel comfortable with the changes they are going through while seeking to change the world. The disciples followed Jesus at the invitation of changing the world. The entire time they were with Jesus, he kept trying to impress upon them that freedom, power, and change are linked to death and service. It appears that as they walked with Jesus they missed the point of his moral and theological teaching, but in the end we know they got it. Jesus responded to their apparent dullness by living his faith in the real world and teaching them to do the same. He provided space for them to grow in their faith in the context of community, and he challenged them to serve others with acts of faith that would change the world as they allowed God to change them.

> They left that place and passed through Galilee. Jesus did not want anyone to know where they were, because he was teaching his disciples. He said to them, "The Son of Man is going to be betrayed into the hands of men. They will kill him, and after three days he will rise." But they did not understand what he meant and were afraid to ask him about it.
>
> They came to Capernaum. When he was in the house, he asked them, "What were you arguing about on the road?" But they kept quiet because on the way they had argued about who was the greatest.
>
> Sitting down, Jesus called the Twelve and said, "If anyone wants to be first, he must be the very last, and the servant of all."
>
> He took a little child and had him stand among them. Taking him in his arms, he said to them, "Whoever welcomes one of these little children in my name welcomes me; and whoever welcomes me does not welcome me but the one who sent me." (Mark 9:30-37 NIV)

The beginning of this passage reflects the disciples' fear to ask Jesus what he meant. Ministry leaders must recognize the fears of young adults and provide a place where they feel safe asking questions. Young adults want to ask questions about things they don't understand but that religious leaders (preachers) take for granted. Jesus, being who he was, recognized the disciples' fear and anticipated their questions. Jesus then gave them a theological principle and applied it, showing them what he meant. Jesus answered their questions by both word and deed. He gave an application and then let them know why the answer mattered.

Just as Jesus was a young adult leading a band of young adults, we see he had to show them what he was talking about by taking a child in his arms. Jesus was talking to them about service and sacrifice that changes the world. They didn't get it, so he went further. You learn what questions young adults have by walking with them and talking with them. Jesus spent a lot time with the disciples in nonteaching settings where he was learning what they were thinking. The theological principle of serving has to be modeled by those who will lead young adult ministries.

As we move along in Mark's Gospel, we realize the disciples are beginning to get understanding. In the end we know they will "get it," because the cross Jesus spoke of becomes real. They see him become the living sacrifice that he predicted he would be, and their faith is increased. Likewise, young adults need to see the connection. They don't like theological abstracts that aren't contextualized in real-world settings. While the disciples saw Jesus' teaching about giving his life realized in front of their eyes, only after the resurrection and the coming of the Spirit did they fully comprehend what Jesus was talking about. So too, young adults may experience pain and disappointment, not fully understanding what they have been taught about their faith. But in a loving community in which they can express their pain and doubts, they can meet the resurrected Christ. In a community in which they can continue to pray and look for Jesus' way, the Spirit can come to them and teach and comfort and empower them to live a new life in an antagonistic world.

Adult developmental theory can predict with a high degree of certainty the changes and challenges young adults will go through. When a ministry informs them about the future they are facing and then equips them to make sense of life with a moral and ethical guide to lead them through the troubled waters, they will draw closer to God and not pull away. This drawing close may or may not immediately increase their Sunday worship attendance, but it will increase their time with God in prayer and study. As they get closer to God and learn how to trust and depend on God, their Sunday worship attendance will increase. Young adults will learn to recognize God's hand in things they see and in situations they go through. When they are given quality biblical instruction that speaks to their present, points to their future, and takes account of their past, they will begin to trust that teaching. Their faith in God and God's Word will multiply.

Doing What Jesus Did with Young Adults

Jesus taught his disciples to observe how God acts in the world through ordinary people and things. Sometimes young adults want to compartmentalize the sacred and the secular; they are trying to put the world in order. But Jesus invites them into this complex and convoluted world and helps them see the wheat among the tares. Jesus can take what appears to be a minor act and transform it into a major meaning-making, faith-forming event. Take, for example, the woman and her small copper coins.

> Jesus sat down opposite the place where the offerings were put and watched the crowd putting their money into the temple treasury. Many rich people threw in large

amounts. But a poor widow came and put in two very small copper coins, worth only a fraction of a penny.

Calling his disciples to him, Jesus said, "I tell you the truth, this poor widow has put more into the treasury than all the others. They all gave out of their wealth; but she, out of her poverty, put in everything—all she had to live on" (Mark 12:41-44 NIV).

In this scene what appeared to be just a regular offering is transformed into a major meaning-making faith act. Jesus intentionally calls the disciples to him. Once they draw close, he helps them make sense of the act as a faith act. The lesson is about sacrifice, service, giving, kingdom ethics, leadership, selflessness, and trust in God. Jesus is urging the disciples, "Look around you and listen to what God is saying." What appears to be an ordinary act can be an act that reflects the will, purpose, and divinity of God. Jesus is teaching his disciples to ask a different set of questions that will help them to find God in their answers.

How or why is God in it? God is in or present with all things because God is omnipresent. The theology of the omnipresence of God and the incarnational principle in Jesus is a theological conundrum, which if taught and understood can assist young adults as they seek to live in a pluralistic society where faith is seen everywhere and nowhere at the same time. They begin to see how God is in every part of their lives. They begin to hear how God is speaking to them not just on Sunday or at Bible study, but always. Teaching such biblical principles to young adults equips them to live empowered lives of faith in the world while not being of the world.

Young adult ministry is rooted in a time of question and development. Just as Jesus walked with his disciples—both men and women—as they traveled along the way, we must do the same thing in young adult ministry. We must pull them aside, walk with them, and respect them as they make their way. They can't be lumped in with the elders, because they aren't there yet. Young adults' journey has to be affirmed, recognized, and respected right where it is and for what it is.

In addition, Jesus made sure the Pharisees didn't get to the disciples. The church must protect young adults from the Pharisees among us while making sure they don't become the next generation of Pharisees. As young adults walk along the way, they are provided space to ask questions and to grow. As they are taught sound doctrine, they will develop a church that will change the world.

A Quest for Identity:
"Who Am I, and What Does All of This Mean?"
by Heidi Donesha Edwards

Heidi Donesha Edwards is a twenty-seven-year-old third-year Master of Divinity student at Fuller Theological Seminary. She received her Bachelor of Arts degree in religious studies from Agnes Scott College.

When I think of young adult ministry, I think of a place I wished that I had as I was *growing* through college. I needed a place in the church where anything was allowed to be asked. My peers and I needed a place where discussions were free and open, with dialogue and engagement with God's Word. Let me tell you a little bit of my story to let you know why I was so eager to ask questions. I was raised in a religiously blended family, that is, a Catholic and Protestant household. And a questioning faith was an anathema. We simply believed, no questions asked. My father was Catholic, and my mother was African Methodist Episcopal. From the outside my household seemed to be a healthy combination of faith and values. Inside the home was a certain amount of turmoil that eventually came to light, and in the midst of this experience, I was looking for somewhere to ask questions of God. But where was that place?

As I entered high school, my longing to become a priest deepened. I got heavily involved in the church and community with various service projects. When I found out one could do ministry and really make a living, I was so excited. To serve God's people as a priest was a dream I refused to let go. As I moved a thousand miles away from home to enter college, I got burnt out with the battle in the church over sexism and the fact that I still hadn't found that place to have faithful, honest dialogue. I had questions about the sovereignty and will of God.

My faith was shaken when my parents divorced, but being far away from home gave me the space and time I need to work through my devastation. I tried to deal with the pain of my family being torn apart but wanted to talk with church leaders about how God could let this happen. I felt alienated from God and from my family. I was like a stranger in a foreign land wandering around lost.

I put everything on the table. My faith was an open book with red markings and questions everywhere. I was questioning everything I had believed and put my trust in. The promises I had believed had been broken; my family was broken; I was broken; the church and the God I had come to believe in had let me down. I needed to ask questions like these: What tradition should I follow? Should I follow the one I inherited from my father—the Catholic Church that wouldn't allow me to be a priest? How much of my abusive past affected my relationships with men and women? What is okay, and what is not okay? Who should I be in loving, intimate relationships with? Are intimate relationships with women a viable option? What are my options? Where do I find love that I can trust?

While asking these questions, I was at a liberal arts college for women where everything seemed permissible. Where was I to turn? I had lost faith and trust in my family's religious tradition and felt utterly alone. I could not talk about these questions with the women whom I had adopted as friends, for they were either ultraconservative Christians or agnostic pagans. I felt as if I were in the dark and couldn't see which way to go.

I thought maybe I could find some direction from my writing, so I wrote. As I read through the journals I kept during that time, I noticed surprisingly that I kept communicating with God. Writing has always been a vehicle for me to talk intimately with God and myself. I asked God these questions and wrote about my struggles. At times I remembered not wanting to write down my experiences; they would send me into shock because the writing made my life seem more vivid than reality. Writing became and still is my personal mirror. I did not want to see what I had gotten myself into—the drinking, promiscuity, and lesbian relationships. I couldn't believe what was happening. I was spiraling out of control while searching for and so wanting control. Where was I to turn?

I remember being deathly afraid of God during this spiral. I just knew that if I died, I would go straight to hell. I cowered at praying, for I felt that it would have been unfair and rude to God if I did. Why pray to God if I continued to live a life contrary to what I had been taught about God? Praying became increasingly harder because I didn't know or understand what God thought about what I was going through. I wanted a word from God, but I did not know how or where to get that word. I wanted to ask God straight up, "Is it okay to be gay? Do you still love me? Can you love me? If you love me at all, why am I going through this? Why did God create me to be the person that I was or was becoming? Did God create me like this? *Who am I?*"

I would cry late into the night as my insides were all torn up. I wanted some support in this confusing time of my life. I turned to a physical relationship as a pacifier to get me through these nights. I thought that if I gave myself to other people and made them feel good about themselves, I would be less likely to go to hell. As quirky as this may sound now, I remember this period like it was yesterday, and I know I wasn't the only one of my peers experiencing this intense struggle. My story isn't as unique as you may think. If you were to take time to talk to young women in college, you would be amazed at how my story is their story. But we don't know this story because we haven't made a place for young adults to tell their stories without shutting them down, shutting them out, or judging them.

My situation got so bad that I eventually decided to seek help. I wanted to go to my family for help, but I couldn't. Being African American from a working-class/middle-class family, I saw some of my issues as an identity question. I thought my questioning was linked to the privileged status I enjoyed as a college student; I was the first in my family to go to college without having gotten pregnant, while still a virgin, and not being married. So I was the chosen or pure one sent to continue the "perfect" life.

Now I find myself sitting with a therapist. My therapist became my confidant. I told her everything. When I finally told her about my relationship with my college roommate, she accepted it. She said that it's okay. I wanted desperately to hear something different. I wanted to hear that it was wrong and that I shouldn't be having these feelings. I wanted to hear that because I wanted to know if this is what God wanted for me in my life. How long would this uncertainty last? What did this mean, and what authority did she have to okay my behavior? I wanted the answer that I would expect from my parents: "No, you are going to hell and must stop your sin at once!"

After "coming out" to my therapist, I told her about the abuse in my life. She then recommended a book for me to read. At this point I was done with therapy. I wanted answers, and she was not delivering! Why would I read a book for therapy if I was seeking her for help? Now I know what I wanted. I wanted a place to work out this stuff in my life. I wanted to sit in a body of believers and cry out and get council and direction from God. I wanted to know what God would say, not what a therapist had to say. I wanted someone to walk with me with integrity and godly wisdom. I didn't need a book; I needed *the* Book, dialogue, support, healthy love, and direction. I stopped therapy, and I started thinking about all of the dreams that I had of being married and having a family. My life was going in a direction that was leading me away from the husband, 2.5 kids, the dog, and the white picket fence. It was as if I heard the voice of God telling me to run, so I ran away from that relationship and toward God. I have not looked back.

My running led me back to the church. I would visit church after church looking for God. Hearing messages about giving your last hundred dollars to a building fund didn't help me. I kept going, looking for God. I was going to ultraconservative churches looking for the correctives I thought I needed. It seemed that if I was not hearing messages about giving, I was hearing messages about pregnant teens followed up by the pastors berating the young women for their "unwanted pregnancies." My head spun, and my next series of relationships spun out of control as well. The church wasn't helping. Now I see how what I was hearing was related to where I was at in my life, but I had yet to find that place to work it all out.

While running to church looking for God and running away from my homosexual relationship, I thought maybe part of the answer was to run to men and look for validation, love, and support. After all, I wasn't gay and I did love men. I met a guy I thought I would marry. The dream was alive again. I had the man of my dreams (or so I thought). I could see the 2.5 kids and the house with the white picket fence. God was faithful; I could trust God again. That relationship turned out not to be the dream come true. Again, I didn't know what was next. All I knew was that whatever was next, God would be there to guide me through. I still have questions, but now I know where to go to find answers.

■ ■ ■

Heidi did find a church that ministers to her where she's at, a church where she can ask questions and work out how to live a Christian life in her complex world. Yet she continues to struggle with past, present, and future. Young adults like Heidi—even when they decide to run away from illicit relationships or drinking or lifestyles that they know are contrary to their faith—continue to wrestle with serious challenges. The answer isn't simply finding the perfect man or woman and nestling into the perfect family that one did not have growing up. The dream husband or dream wife doesn't exist! How can the church help young adults sort our fantasy from real life and then make their way in real life? The church has to start by listening to their stories and taking their struggles and questions seriously. Then together we can take the issues of their lives to the Word of God and find the answers to those questions.

QUESTIONS TO CONSIDER

1. Where are your young adults?
2. What questions do they have about life?
3. What questions do they have about faith?
4. What questions do they have about the Bible?
5. How do they understand their purpose and call?
6. How do they understand the purpose of prayer?
7. What do they know about prayer?
8. Do they know how to discern the voice of God from their own voice?
9. Are they equipped with the tools to study the Bible?
10. What questions do they have about sexuality?
11. What questions do they have about relationships?
12. How many of them have been abused?

13. How many of them are in jobs they hate?

14. How many are struggling with relationships with their parents or nuclear or extended family?

15. What are they getting out of coming to worship?

16. What teaching style fits their lifestyle? (This is a congregational issue as well as a generational issue.)

17. Where are they allowed to ask questions and not be ashamed?

18. How is the church protecting them from the Pharisees?

19. To what extent are they seeing the power of God in their lives and the life of the church?

20. Biblically, why is it important to have a young adult ministry?

NOTES

1. J. P. Moreland and Mark Matlock, *Smart Faith: Loving Your God with All Your Mind* (Downers Grove, IL: InterVarsity, 2003), 23.

2. Robin Sylvan, *Traces of the Spirit: The Religious Dimensions of Popular Music* (New York: New York University Press, 2002), 3–5.

3. Ibid., 5.

4. Michael Muhammad Knight, *The Five Percenters: Islam, Hip-Hop and The Gods of New York* (England: Oneworld Publications, 2007).

5. Sharon Daloz Parks, *Big Questions, Worthy Dreams: Mentoring Young Adults in Their Search for Meaning, Purpose, and Faith* (San Francisco: Jossey-Bass, 2000), 21.

6. Ibid., 35.

3

Growing Up to Be Free:
The Developmental Phases
of Young Adults

When I was a child, I spoke as a child, I understood
as a child, I thought as a child; but when I became
a man [or woman], I put away childish things.
1 CORINTHIANS 13:11

To put it simply, young adults are trying to grow up. They are trying to become full-fledged independent functioning adults. In the
move from adolescence to adult, they need to define themselves in
relationship to what their parents have pressed on them. So they are
now trying to press back and take charge of their own identity. This
press is not a battle of good versus evil, but is a tug-o-war for
redefining the relationship. These budding adults are no longer
children, so questions arise of who are they and how they relate
to their elders. How do they relate to themselves, their parents,
their friends, their God, and their church? This is just the tip of the
iceberg regarding the development of young adults. Another way
we can talk about this life transition is to examine the developmental phases of young adults.

Young adults will go through distinguishable developmental phases—characterized by age categories and life transitions—that can be charted. According to Gail Sheehy, these stages of young adult development can be broken into two major categories.[1] The first category is ages eighteen to thirty, which Sheehy defines as a period of provisional adulthood. In this period youth are becoming young adults. Sheehy refers to this period as the "try-out twenties." It is a time of trying new things and seeking to locate oneself, one's identity, one's likes, and one's dislikes in terms of relationships, vocation, and faith. The second major grouping is ages thirty to forty-five, or first adulthood. Sheehy calls this period the "turbulent thirties" (though she sees this as extending into the early forties). It is a time of discovery and confusion. Young adults tend to settle down around thirty-five as they begin their life quest, which leads to what Sheehy calls the "flourishing forties."

We will break down each phase into smaller segments to help you understand what young adults are going through developmentally. Understanding the challenges young adults experience in each phase of transition will help you better understand how to serve with them in ministry and minister to them. In the next chapter we will talk about how to minister to each phase of transition.

Life Phase Eighteen to Twenty-five: "Who I Be?"

The first phase of development for young adults is the stage between the ages of eighteen and twenty-five. This phase is typically referred to as the college years, but we refer to it as the "Who I be?" phase. For many African Americans this phase does not include college. It may include finding that first real full-time job and/or going to a vocational school or junior college.

When we think about today's African American young adults, we have to be mindful of the era to which they belong. They are

31

the first generation to grow up watching music television and the history channel and surfing the Internet. This generation has the largest percentage of any generation raised outside of the church. This generation defines themselves by labels (Phat Farm, Sean John, etc.). They are divided by an ever-expanding class divide. They saw crack addiction be replaced by meth. They watched a U.S. president's extramarital affair play out in the news and a televangelist go by the same sin. They are suspicious of the church and leadership, whom, in many instances, they see as failing them.

DMX came out with a song on his third compact disc titled "Who We Be." The chorus includes this famous line: "They don't know who we be." The "they" is vague, but one could infer he is talking about the dominant culture. In response to this song, I always ask, do *we* know who we are? Working with young adults in the church and on college campuses, we find this to be the most pressing question in the life of young adults during this life phase. Who am I in relationship to my nuclear family, extended family, friends, intimate relationships, ethnic identity, and yes, my faith? The quest for an interdependent identity presses upon them as they try to make sense of where they have come from and where they are going.

This initial period of transition and transformation for African American young adults requires them to work out who they are apart from their immediate family. For the first eighteen years of their lives, they have been told what to do, where to go, and what time to come in; now they have to begin making these decisions for themselves in the context of a world they have to negotiate without the immediate oversight of their parents or extended family. This is especially the case for young adults who move out of the house where they were raised and establish their own residence. It is also the case for young adults who go off to college.

The key work during this phase is helping young adults begin to ask questions about identity and purpose. These are hard questions at this stage, as they are afraid and confused about who they are and what their adult lives should look like. But they must begin to ask these difficult questions. This is a time of laying the broad strokes of independence and adult identity construction. Parents who hold on too tightly during this phase by providing too much support and direction can get in the way of the process. Parents/guardians must be encouraged to let go and let the young adults grow, and be supported in this change in their role. This also is a word to young adult ministry. Young adult ministry isn't youth ministry. Young adults must be empowered to define and grow their ministry as leaders with elders' support, not oversight.

So we have these young adults who are acting youthful while looking like adults and at times acting like adults. Then there are moments when childlike characteristics rear their heads and they don't know which way to go. Equally confused, the parents/guardians don't know which way to go either. They wonder, *How am I to treat him [or her]—like an adult or a child?* They don't need chaperones, but they would welcome trusted, loving mentors who are willing to walk with them through this confusing period.

Young adults don't know who they are, and who they will become has yet to become manifest. They are working this out publicly and can't hide the changes. They don't want to be told who they should be by older adults. They want to find this out for themselves. The role of the church, and especially young adult ministry, is to recognize the journey they are on and walk with them through this period. The life decisions they make will shape the answers to the questions they are asking and forever shape the direction of their lives. To this end young adults are exploring that danger zone of being almost grown while not knowing what "grown" feels like or looks like. Ministering to their dreams and visions is important. Encouraging them to pursue their dreams and helping them find means to making their God-given dreams or visions a reality has to be one of the central concerns of ministry to this population of young adults.

This first phase of young adulthood has been labeled prolonged adolescence. African American young adults are staying home longer and needing to depend on their nuclear family for support well into their twenties. The age-old idea of growing up and leaving is more of a coming and going phenomena. They are caught in a tenuous position: "What is my address?" They have an intense desire to be free, but they can't afford it! The desire to break away from family in an effort to define oneself is muted by the need for physical, emotional, and financial support from their elders. Therefore the identities of young adults are filled with mixed messages and mixed emotions.

This "who we be" phase is a period of fear and anxiety. Questions abound: What does tomorrow hold? How can I hold it together? Can I do this? What if I fail? What should I do? Where should I go? Where should I live? Where do I want to live? What do I call my parents? Do I still want to go to church? Do I believe in God? Do I believe in the church? Should I have sex? What do I really want to do with my life? Who am I now that I'm out of high school? Do I really have the authority to say who I am?

This first phase of young adulthood is not only a confusing and trying time for the young adults, but also for their primary caregivers. Parents need to be assisted in letting go and being conscious of what their young adults are going through. In fact, churches might do well to have a support group that ministers to parents of young adults. If parents interfere too much, they can disrupt this period of transformation and retard the "growing up" of young adults. Parents have to let their young adults go without letting them fall. They have to push them out of the nest without pushing them over the edge. This is a difficult and delicate balance that needs to be entered into with common sense and prayer.

Since this is the most critical stage of setting young adults on the path for future success, the church must come alongside families and help get young adults pointed in the right direction. For unless these years are negotiated successfully, many young adults and their families will find themselves trying to work out the first-phase issues in the next phase of development. That can become the equivalent of starting late in the race.

Life Phase Twenty-six to Thirty-five: "I Know Who I Am—I Think!"

If the church and their families have supported young adults through the previous phase, they have come into their own. They have wrestled openly and honestly with questions of faith, purpose, and identity. An initial career path for this phase of adulthood is set in view. This career path may be questioned down the road, but for now they enjoy an initial comfort with where they are and where they are going. It is time we let them not only take the reins in young adult ministry, but also get involved in the larger leadership scheme of the church.

In this period a young adult's long-term relationship with a significant other is likely going through one of two extremes. Either it is moving toward marriage or it is being reconsidered and terminated. Waves in male-female relationships are predictable during this period, so the ministry needs to come alongside young adults with relational support. As they leave their twenties and enter their thirties, they face the reality that they aren't the "young" ones anymore. As the pressure of intimate relationships, career, children, and the church weigh on them, the church must find ways to support them in this stage of their journey. They are moving toward that dreaded middle age—an age they thought they would never reach. A reminder to them that they are not middle-aged may be helpful; there is a lot of time left to pursue life goals and even change career paths if they are so led. Even if they didn't do all the work they could have or should have done in the previous phase, they still have time.

Young adults need intense, intentional development of the spiritual disciplines during this phase. The spiritual disciplines of prayer, fasting, study of God's Word, journaling, and meditation are central. The point of these disciplines is to help them learn how to reflect and discern the will of God in their lives as they move through this critical stage that sets them up for the next phase in life—when they move from being young adults to adults. The big 4-0 is on the horizon, and that will become another intense moment as they move out of this phase of development. A return to the issue of calling resurfaces in the mid-forties. After having been on an initial career path for a number of years or bouncing around in jobs, now comes a time of asking what one really wants to do with the rest of his or her life. This is a question that can only be answered well in conversation with God, so it is important to empower young adults with tools to hear and recognize God's voice.

Life Phase Thirty-six to Forty: "Am I Really This Old?"

The mid- to late thirties is a time of settling. This is a sobering time for young adults. If they have done the work of the previous stage, they are settled in a career, are paying back student loans, may have a small family, and may be looking at buying their first home while dealing with car payments. For those from more working-class backgrounds, paying student loans isn't an issue. They are working to maintain their job, pay rent, keep insurance on their car, or keep their bus pass paid. Their future is less secure than it may be for those who have gone to college and found themselves on a settled career path. With the number of African American males going to college dwindling, while the numbers going to prison are increasing, this period of life can be a mixed bag in the African American church. The enormous class divide in the African American community must be taken into account at all stages of development, but in this stage it is especially important to consider the different trajectories among young adults so that the ministry meets the needs of all.

In the earlier stages of development, all young adults were struggling with identity questions and trying to secure a firm foundation for their future. They had dreams and visions for their future. Those privileged enough to have laid a foundation for those dreams are starting to see the fruit of their labor. Those who have fought to this point to survive are having a hard time dealing with the realization that their dreams may not become a reality. Those who haven't had the opportunity to fulfill their dreams can get caught in a cycle of longing, waiting for their dream to come like a thief in the night. Following the revival and religious speakers' circuit where the message "Your blessing is coming tomorrow" is preached becomes their "fix." Despair and depression can also be a part of this period for those who buy into "woulda', coulda', shoulda' " talk. "See, what happened was…And all I got to do is…" They are in denial that nothing is happening, so conversation that avoids dealing with reality pacifies them.

At this critical stage of development, the ministry to young adults has to be even more vigilant. The weight of children, relationships, and bills is staring them in the face. They are trying to make that move into their early forties, not thinking they would ever be this old, and they will either look back and be proud, or on the other extreme, look back and wonder why they didn't get done what they wished they had. "I thought I would be further along by now," they say. Now they really look like fully grown adults. They are walking and talking like they have it all together. They are being integrated with those in their fifties and sixties, but their life is at a different stage than the older church members. At this stage in life, the church has to help them to look critically at where they have been and where they are going while helping them map out a plan to get there. This a time for practical, hands-on life directional ministry. They continue to search for purpose and concrete direction as how to make what's next happen. They are looking to the church and God to show them not simply what is next but how to get there. This is a two-track ministry at the minimum.

The first track of this ministry period is focused on working with those who don't feel as if they have realized their dreams to date and don't see how they are going to realize them in the future. The second track is for those who feel as if they haven't made sufficient progress in the area of their life dreams and are now trying to reposition themselves for greater things, because as successful as they feel, they are asking, "Is this all there is? Is there more to life than this?" They are seeking to be fulfilled in new and different ways, and they are finding that career success and money are not the be all and end all. So in the case of both those who are successful and those who had hoped for more of a sense of success, there is a void that needs to be filled and ministered to via the young adult ministry.

Young adult ministry has to understand the phases of development that young adults are in and affirm their periods of transition. They have a lot going on and can easily get mixed up. The ministry has to help them disentangle and make sense of their lives and realize that what they are going through isn't a bad thing or a weird thing. What young adults are going through is as normal as what adolescents go through. If young adults are given license to experience the transition, they will not think it strange as they ask questions and seek guidance.

"Making Hollywood My Mission Field":
Connecting Faith and Journey
by Colleen Yvonne Thomas

Colleen is pursuing a Master of Arts in Theology with a concentration in theology and art at Fuller Theological Seminary. At twenty-seven, Colleen has realized her gifting as a singer-songwriter and is presently at work on a recording project. Her love of God, of music, and for entertainers compels her toward a career in the music industry.

At twenty-seven years of age, I find myself at crossroads. One way is living out my dream of becoming an artist in Hollywood, and the other is "settling into reality." The pressures are immense. And because I am the daughter of parents who did what was expected of most in their generation of baby boomers—graduate from college if they could, strive for financial security via a good stable job, get married, have children, buy a house—my life is often lived without much support. Artists are typically unsupported by society at large, not just family. We are the vagabonds of modern society—we live without health care insurance, benefits, and 401(k) plans. Even I find myself wondering if I should give it all up and put my expensive degree from New York University into action. Especially conflicting are my thoughts as a young Christian woman pursuing a career as a singer in Hollywood. Can you imagine the pressure?

Most of my friends are artists, and I find it quite interesting that our parents' generation is so baffled by the artistic desire present in so many of us, their children. I've had many conversations with confused parents of friends and family who don't get why their child won't just pick a career or finish college. The parents cannot identify with our artistic passions. But I venture to guess it is not that they themselves cannot understand what it feels like to have a passion for something burning deep inside themselves. I believe we get our artistic passions from them. Rather, they struggle to identify with the freedom our generation exercises in choosing a life lived with no certain outcome.

To be a Christian artist in Hollywood is to live a life of faith. My calling and my faith are what compel me, despite the many opinions surrounding the life of Christians in "secular" arts fields. And it is about this concern that I now write because it is a source of much contention in our churches.

There is a deep spirit of despair in Hollywood, dressed up in beautiful images and smiling before cameras for photos that adorn magazine covers. Christians also are inundated by images of fame and fortune. We turn glossy pages of celebrity magazines and begin to disassociate celebrities from their human spiritual need for a word of reconciliation. And just like that, as we lust after the secrets and rewards of the success of those celebrities, the enemy succeeds in resigning us from our roles as ambassadors for Christ. It becomes difficult to see that these Hollywood people who look like they have it all are, without Christ, much like Nicodemus. Here was a man of great stature, but he was in need of a Savior. He was a man of power and influence, but he knew he needed more. He needed Jesus—and so do the rich and famous and powerful in Hollywood. So when I am asked about my role as a young Christian woman in Hollywood (or an artist in America in general), I respond that it is a life lived out of faith. And this is what I would tell parents of a child with artistic passion: to be an artist is a high calling, for it calls you to live a missional and prophetic life. Often we as Christian artists segregate ourselves culturally from the "secular" arts world out of fear, which results in our ministering only to one another through song or poetry or dance. Yet if we all continue to express our gifts only in church, who will be out there in Hollywood forming relationships with other entertainers and celebrities? Who will be there to plead with God on their behalf?

When Jesus spoke to the disciples about the challenge it would be for a rich man to enter into the kingdom of God and said it would be easier for a camel to go through the eye of a needle, the disciples were amazed and asked him, "Who then can be saved?" Christ responded by saying, "With men this is impossible, but with God all things are possible" (Matthew 19:23-26). Jesus left a huge window of possibility open—and a great door of responsibility.

As artists, we take our gifts seriously. In Hollywood one treats his or her art as a business. As Christians, we take our calling seriously. To be an ambassador for Christ in Hollywood is a serious undertaking. Yet God only asks of us willingness. Sure, some developed disciplines will come in handy, such as a deep faith in God through Christ, a personal commitment to spiritual disciplines, knowledge of spiritual warfare, operation of spiritual gifts, and a great love for all creation, art, and culture.

QUESTIONS TO CONSIDER

1. In what stages are young adults in your church, and how should this affect the programming and ministry that you provide?

2. What percentage of your young adults are in each developmental phase?

a. Stage #1 (18–25):

b. Stage #2 (26–35):

c. Stage #3 (36–40):

3. What support does the young adult ministry provide for the parents and guardians of young adults?

4. What type of relationship support/counseling does your young adult ministry provide for young adults who are trying to deal with love and issues of intimate relationships?

5. What type of relationship models that young adults can touch does your young adult ministry have in the church?

6. What type of career counseling or coaching does your ministry provide?

7. How do your young adults understand their identity and purpose in life?

8. How does your young adult ministry help young adults deal with the practical concerns of each phase of development?

a. Male-female relationships

b. Sex versus celibacy

c. Family and friends network—who should I hang with and who should I cut off?

d. Financial issues

e. Moving in or out of the house—dealing with "Mommanem"

f. Moving from youth church to being integrated into the adult life of the church and having the respect of other adults

NOTES

1. This grouping and its characteristics are taken from Gail Sheehy, *New Passages: Mapping Your Life across Time* (New York: Random House, 1995); see also Bakari Kitwana, *The Hip Hop Generation: Young Blacks and the Crisis in African American Culture* (New York: Basic Civitas Books, 2003).

4.

Ministering to the Phases:
A Model for Young Adult Ministry

> And at this point His disciples came, and they
> marveled that He talked with a woman; yet no
> one said, "What do You seek?" or, "Why are
> You talking with her?" The woman then left her
> waterpot, went her way into the city, and said to
> the men, "Come, see a Man who told me all
> things that I ever did. Could this be the Christ?"
> Then they went out of the city and came to Him.
>   JOHN 4:27-30

The story of Jesus' encounter with the woman at the well provides
us with at least two lessons for young adult ministry. The first
thing we can learn comes from the part of the story we didn't
quote, John 4:7-9, where Jesus asks the woman to give him a
drink. In essence she had something to offer Jesus. We suggest in
this chapter and in chapter 7 that young adults have something to
offer the church. The second lesson is that after the woman met
Jesus and found out who he was, she took this word to the city
and brought the people to see a man who told her all the things
she had done. She was actively involved in growing the ministry.

We suggest in this chapter that young adults must be involved in birthing, leading, and growing their ministry.

This chapter is not meant to be prescriptive so much as descriptive. Our intent is to give practical examples that embrace the principles to inform the development of a young adult ministry in your church. These examples can be modified to fit your context.

Birthing the Young Adult Ministry

Birthing a successful young adult ministry requires that young adults be a part of the process from start to finish. As we said earlier, they are not looking for chaperones, but for mentors. The birthing process needs a mentor-leader who is appointed by the senior pastor. This should be a person who can serve as minister to young adults or in a similar capacity, such as director of young adult ministries. This person does not need to be a minister, but he or she must have a love and passion for young adults and must understand and be sensitive to the transitions young adults go through. This person must be called to walk with young adults as they navigate their journey. He or she may be a member of the young adult peer group, but if this is the case, he or she must be a mature member. The leader may be older than the young adult peer group but, again, must see his or her role as a mentor and not a chaperone. Young adults are no longer members of the youth group, and they will not tolerate being treated as if they are still in the youth group. In the process of birthing the ministry, young adults must have a significant degree of control and input facilitated by the designated organizer.

The first step in developing a young adult ministry is to bring a core group of young adults together to begin the planning process. This can be done one of two ways. One way is to make an open call for young adults to come to an organizational meeting. Another way is to strategically select a core group of young adults who have proven themselves as leaders and appoint them to oversee the birthing process. There may be other ways to birth such a ministry, but in our experience these two ways, or some hybrid of them, have worked best. The principle here is involving the young adults. This initial group should be involved in developing the mission statement for the ministry, which must coincide with and support the general church mission statement. It is good to bring to this first meeting a draft of a mission statement for them to respond to.

Having a broad representative base from the church at the first meeting is important. And young adults must be encouraged to take ownership of the group from the start. You do this by involving them, listening to them, and addressing the issues they are raising. The person leading this gathering must be someone young adults can relate to and who takes them seriously. This person must be sensitive to their needs and be able to hear them without being critical or dismissive. Young adults will come to this meeting already feeling, in many instances, as if the church has not heard them, so the church must earn their trust and let them know that they are seen as adults who have a voice and power when it comes to developing a ministry. The initial group of leaders will shape the direction of the ministry and will also serve as the "poster child" for how the ministry is perceived by the church and other young adults.

Being as strategic as possible when selecting this initial group is important, for they will speak to two important constituencies: the young adults themselves and the larger adult church. The diversity of young adults in the church or on the college campus and those outside the church you are trying to attract must see themselves in this ministry from the beginning. As you choose the initial group of leaders, it is vital that it be diverse in terms of educational background, class, age, and gender, so be as representative as you can. The initial group of leaders will be the face of the ministry.

The larger adult church who will need to embrace and support this ministry will be watching. With the divide between young adults and older adults being aggravated by the debate around hip-hop, it is important to bring the older adults along. The senior pastor is key, for the senior pastor has to walk beside the young adults to protect them while preparing the church to embrace them. The divide between the elders and young adults cannot be taken lightly, for the concerns are serious. There will also be a power struggle in the life of the church as the young adults represent the future leadership of the church. The older adults will recognize this emerging new leadership base and react. Since young adult ministry represents *change*, the senior pastor and church leaders have to be prepared to integrate young adults into the life of the larger church, which means facilitating and leading the change process. Young adult ministry can't be put on the side or on the outside of the church; it must be an integral part of the life of the larger church.

Locating Young Adult Ministry at the Center of Church Life

The church must fight the tendency to treat young adult ministry like some churches treat youth ministry. In some churches youth ministry is put in a warehouse or some other building labeled as a youth area. The youth don't worship with the larger church or fellowship with their elders; they are left alone. Being "left alone" means that they aren't touched by or in touch with the larger adult church. They are not integrated and developed by the elders. As my Fuller Theological Seminary colleague Dr. Chap Clark says, "Youth ministry is treated like the ear of Mickey Mouse." The head of Mickey Mouse is the "real church," and youth ministry sits off to the side. Not a part of the "real church," it protrudes like an ill-placed left ear.

The church has to fight the tendency to treat young adult ministry like the other ear of Mickey Mouse. Young adults have something to offer the church. They challenge the way things are done and breathe new life into the church. If they are left outside, they will still have energy, but it won't influence the life of the larger church. In order to energize the whole church, young adults must be a part of the total life of the church, including worship. They shouldn't be relegated to "young adult Sunday"; they need to be a part of every Sunday. Thus a church that is serious about ministry to all ages needs to be cognizant of how they worship and whether their worship is relevant for youth, young adults, and older adults. If this principle of inclusion isn't taken seriously, a church might have a vibrant young adult ministry that isn't reflected on Sunday mornings. Young adults will support the young adult ministry but maybe not the larger church.

To avoid this trap, the young adult ministry must from the outset be built with the intent of integrating the ministry and young adults into the life of the total church. How do you do integration? We believe you have to start by asking the right questions from the beginning. As your church embarks on building a young adult ministry, you should consider the following fifteen points.

    1. Define what you mean by the term "young adults." Make sure your definition has an age component and faith development component.

    2. Determine what age ranges you will include in your ministry. What will be your focus age ranges to start with? You may have to start from your strength or largest young adult population group. Or you may want to start with a college outreach ministry. There is also the possibility of starting a mass young adult group and letting the subgroups emerge. The key is defining your focus early.

3. Find your young adults. Where are they in your congregation and community? Locate their centers of activity and interest and use that information to determine how your ministry can reach them.

4. Know your population. Who are the young adults in your church and community? Do your research. This research has to be internal and external. A good source is MAP (Ministry Area Profile; http://www.perceptgroup.com/Products/MinistryArea Profile/MAPfront.aspx).

5. Start with their needs in mind. Survey them and publish your findings. It is important to systematically find out what they want (see survey sample in Appendix A).

6. Once you survey the young adults, respond to their needs. Don't judge them or try to tell them what they need. Listen and take seriously what they say they need and want.

7. Collect data at every chance you get; whenever the young adults are together, get more data. Invite them to evaluate everything. Let them know that their evaluation counts by responding to their evaluations. They must know that their voice matters.

8. Keep the young adults in the loop at every turn. Don't leave them out and make unilateral decisions. Even if you don't do what they want, at least explain to them the rationale for your decisions.

9. Communicate quickly. Young adults want to know right away about everything, so use technology (e-mail, text, podcast, video streaming, etc.).

10. Make sure your ministry has a steady rudder (e.g., Bible study or some systematic, regular engagement with God's Word) and is activity focused at the same time. Young adults respond to events that make a difference, so events must be "hot" and engaging. Young adults are looking for quality!

11. Ask your leaders the following questions: How are we going to minister to young adults outside of the "young adult ministry"? Is our worship speaking to them? How does our order of service include them? Is our music relevant to them? Do they feel at home in worship?

12. Consider how young adults can play a part in church leadership.

13. Think about how you can develop young adults to become stewards, deacons, trustees, elders, and leaders in the church.

14. Evaluate how your Christian education program speaks to the challenges young adults are facing in life.

15. Consider how much access young adults have to your senior pastor. Are you relegating the care of young adults to the young adult pastor and sending a message that the senior pastor isn't really their pastor?

The church leadership team needs to talk about these issues, and they need to include young adults in the conversation. Thinking through these fifteen points will help you to think before you act. If they are addressed prior to start-up, the ministry will have a better chance of succeeding. It is critical that a new young adult ministry not fail, because if it does, that will dash the little faith young adults have in the church.

Developing a Ministry that Touches All Young Adults

The phases that young adults are going through must be considered as the ministry is being developed. Young adult ministry can be broken up into three major divisions related directly to the stages of development young adults go through: the "trying twenties," the traditional college-age years; the late twenties through the "turbulent thirties"; and the late thirties through the "flour-ishing forties." As we discussed in chapter 3, each of these stages includes particular challenges that should be the focus of your ministry. Therefore the phases of life that young adults are going through must be considered as the outreach begins. With this in mind, we offer the following suggestions.

Collegiate Ministry or Traditional College-Age Ministry: The Trying Twenties

Establishing a partnership between your young adult ministry and the college office of student development or student activities is a must. The local church doesn't want to be seen as a competing ministry, but rather as a partner ministry. The local church can establish a ministry on campus with the approval and support of the office of student development or student activities, or it can partner with an existing campus organization. This is a contextual issue, and one is as good as the other as long as you consider your context. Residential colleges are places where young adults are searching for answers to questions such as these: Who am I in relationship to the home I left behind? How do I define myself, my faith, and my relationship to God? How will I live out my faith in this context? These questions of identity and relationship to God are driving what they are struggling with. Bible studies and activities that speak directly to these questions while allowing young adults the latitude to wrestle with them are important. Using popular culture as a springboard for conversation is a good way to get them involved in the dialogue. You want them talking to you (the leader), each other, and God. This is a time when they can't wait to talk. They have been listening in church for a long time, and they don't want to put their hands up anymore. They want to shout out. On the other hand, they have a lot of questions about their new life that they want answered.

In these years there tends to be two extremes: "college Christians gone wild" versus "going wild for Christ." The tension in these two extremes should be the focus of the collegiate or college-age ministry—that is, we need to be walking with young adults as they try to navigate this tension. They must be encouraged to talk about this tension without judging one another. You may find that those who have gone wild for Jesus can be very judgmental of those who have simply gone wild. You may also meet former youth group kids who don't want anything to do with the Christians on campus for any number of reasons. The ministry to young adults in this stage must appeal to the unchurched, the unsaved, former youth group kids who either want to not do church or to recreate youth group, and young adults who don't want anything to do with the on-campus zealots. Remember, this is the time of trying things out; young adults are trying things and trying to find themselves. Collegiate ministry is a tough job because the constituencies are so wide and the ministry is continually being examined under a microscope.

In the case of college ministry, make sure you reach out to campus leaders and allow them to be the face of the ministry. Peer leadership is crucial on college campuses and with college-age young adults. They follow their leaders faster than they will follow an older adult who invades their campus. The young adult minister who is a part of the college environment is seen as a type of professor, and the relationship between student and faculty member is a model that young adults are used to on the college campus. In the areas of faith development, as well as in the best of classrooms, there is a mix between lecture and dialogue. Young adults don't want to be preached to or talked down to. They want to be involved in the conversation. It is okay to hold them responsible for their learning and development. It is okay to involve them in the teaching as student teachers—after all, the ministry is meant to develop them to lead the church.

The church that attracts young adults on Sundays must have a Sunday component that recognizes them and meets their needs.

They are looking for something that says "Welcome" (see Nicole Watkins's reflections in chapter 5). Make sure worship speaks to them in tangible ways. Welcome them and make arrangements to minister to them after worship in the form of some type of fellowship. Something as simple as a monthly meal together can make a difference. Also, something like a lunch bag for them to take back to campus filled with a memory verse, a gift certificate to a fast-food restaurant, some cookies, and a worship CD can make a major difference. The key is letting them know that you care and that you are responding to their needs in tangible ways.

The Turbulent Thirties: "Say What?"

Thirty is the new twenty.

—Jay-Z

Young adults in their late twenties and early thirties need a ministry that allows them to emerge as leaders. They see themselves as young, but not like the college-age set. In fact, to some extent the title "young adult" is suspect, as they are moving out of this phase. The ministry has to work at helping them walk in both worlds—the world of young adult ministry and the larger church ministry as adults. This role of young adult ministry to this age group is best described as a bridge ministry. People in this age group will lead in developing the programming they need, but the church has to be ready to step up to the plate and respond. Budget issues will be a point of debate, as the ministry will have to be supported financially by the church.

Young adults don't always give a lot financially to the church for a variety of reasons. Perhaps some don't give because they are establishing a life and have a lot of financial demands. Or perhaps they don't give much because they haven't matured in their faith to the point of being tithers. In this case, the church must be prepared to support the ministry financially while at the same time growing young adults into givers. The teaching of spiritual disciplines is critical at this point in their faith development.[1] Remember that your job is to develop them into the leaders they are destined to become. If the work of developing their faith and their giving is done during this stage, the church will have a solid leadership base for its future.

The Flourishing Forties: "I'm All Grown Up Now!"
Thirty is the same old thirty.
—Lyfe Jennings
The last phase of young adult ministry is graduation from the young adult ranks. They are moving out of their first adulthood into their second adulthood. This is a sobering move. During this phase of ministry, it is important to help young adults realize that they have a lot of life left, and as they now move to the head of the class, it is time for them to take over. It is time for them to become full-fledged leaders in the church. If the ministry has done its job in the previous phases, they are settled and ready to lead. The turbulent times of the twenties and thirties have been negotiated. Now they will lead the programming and funding of the ministry. In fact, they will be insulted if the church doesn't hold them accountable for supporting the ministry. They are also expecting to be integrated as leaders in the larger church. They don't want to wait on the sidelines; they want to be in the game. The church must be ready to meet this expectation and put them in the places God has prepared for them.

■ ■ ■

Birthing a young adult ministry is not something that can be relegated to the young adult pastor or director. The entire church must be led by the senior pastor to get their arms around this ministry and bring young adults in with love. Young adults are looking for strong, loving, mentoring relationships in the church. This need can be met only as the body of Christ as a whole takes this charge seriously. A plan to grow the ministry, integrate young adults into the life of the larger church, and transition young adults to full adults must all be a part of your church's short-term and long-term vision.

"What Don't Work?"
A Reflection on a College Ministry
That Didn't Reach the Next Level
by Charles Dorsey

Charles was a part of a ministry that focused on college students and wasn't as concerned about the larger young adult population. He shares why it is important when you start or as you grow your young adult ministry to be mindful of the bigger young adult picture.

Real success as a Christian leader is developing a movement that can be sustained after God has called you to other levels of service. One of the most difficult tasks for a leader is prioritizing the time to develop a person or group of people who will replace you. In the midst of developing relationships, being creative, negotiating faith, and maintaining zeal, attention is easily removed from the necessity to prepare for the future. The easiest decision for a Christian leader is to avoid the complication of developing other leaders by managing all the responsibility on your own. By doing this, however, you set up your ministry for abrupt and devastating failure.

This was exactly the case, in the fall of 2006, during my graduating year at the University of California at Irvine. I was fortunate to have been able to found a young adult gospel choir in 2001 and watch it grow from six to forty members and to help birth a Bible study with consistent attendance. I had become so consumed by the idea of immediate success that I had no time for developing other leaders. The fear of expecting other people to duplicate my own work ethic, the reality of reduced volunteer personnel, and the attachment that I had created through long hours of dedication created a sense of personal responsibility to this ministry and made it easier to depend on myself more than others. Graduation crept into my consciousness, and the panic of unprepared succession began to affect my optimistic vision for this ministry. Who would take my place after I graduated? Was anyone interested and willing to accept the burden and success of this ministry? If no one volunteered, this young adult ministry was going cease to exist regardless of all the positive contributions it made to the campus. My heart was burdened by these possibilities, while God provided an opportunity to learn a valuable lesson about transition and leadership.

The pulpit has historically demonstrated that Christian leaders accept positions of service with the expectancy of long-term residence. Many successful ministries have found themselves under the same leaders for decades, which would seemingly indicate how young adult ministries are to be initiated and maintained. This long-term paradigm, however, is not applicable in the twenty-first-century young adult ministry context. The success of a young adult ministry depends on the leaders' willingness and ability to deal with the burden of transition. This burden is the fact that youth and young adult leaders and participants eventually matriculate through school, which the church aggressively encourages. Consequently, how is one expected to sustain young adult ministry?

The fast-paced atmosphere of young adult ministry demands a consistent development process of on-coming leaders. You cannot be the only person with leadership responsibility and expect your ministry to endure transition. One of the pivotal mistakes I made in my young adult ministry was underestimating the potential of its participants. Success in young adult ministry requires an acknowledgment of the consistent transition that occurs in the lives of young people and a willingness to empower them with the responsibility to lead, maintain, and reproduce young adult ministry. A young adult ministry leader who mismanages authority by neglecting the development of a successor handicaps and shortens the life of their ministry. Are you prepared for transition?

QUESTIONS TO CONSIDER

1. What do we mean when we say "young adult"?

2. What age ranges will our young adult ministry serve?

3. What age range should we focus on as we start the young adult ministry?

4. Where are young adults active in the church?

5. Where are young adults active in our city?

6. How will we use technology to communicate quickly and efficiently with our young adult population?

7. How will we include the young adult leadership team in the larger leadership structure of the church?

8. How does our Christian education ministry speak to the life stages young adults are going through?

9. How will the senior pastor stay in touch with and close to the young adult ministry?

10. How will the church give tangible support to the young adult leadership team?

NOTES

1. Richard Foster, *Celebration of Discipline: The Path to Spiritual Growth* (San Francisco: Harper & Row, 1978).

5

The Young Adult Struggle: Between a Rock and a Hard Place

"But after I have been raised, I will go before you to Galilee."

Peter answered and said to Him, "Even if all are made to stumble because of You, I will never be made to stumble."

Jesus said to him, "Assuredly, I say to you that this night, before the rooster crows, you will deny Me three times."

Peter said to Him, "Even if I have to die with You, I will not deny You!" And so said all the disciples.

MATTHEW 26:32-35

In many ways this story about Peter typifies the experience of young adults in their faith walk. Peter is trying to figure out what it means to follow Christ, and he goes from one extreme to the other. In this passage Peter expresses a radical commitment, but Jesus, understanding Peter's struggle and being the perfect minister to young adults, tells him what he is going to do. Peter doesn't stop there, as we know: he cuts off the ear of the high priest's servant (Matthew 26:51). But then he swings to the opposite extreme and denies Jesus in Matthew 26:69-75. We can condemn Peter, or we can understand that for Peter and his peers this was a confusing time. They were trying to make sense of their lives, Jesus' ministry, and this whole suffering servant, crucifixion, resurrection thing. It was a lot to put together. This is coupled with the fact that they had chosen to leave their old lives for this new life, and they probably didn't think it was going to end like this.

Peter and the other disciples were between a rock and a hard place and found themselves asking: "What do I do now?" "Who do I trust?" "How do I carve out my future?" "Do I go back to fishing?" "Do I try to keep teaching what Jesus has taught us?" "Was he really the Messiah?" "Was this all real, or was it a hoax?" Peter and the other disciples, homeboys along with the women who were around Jesus, like young adults today, find themselves caught in a web of big questions linked with their faith journey. And they don't have easy answers.

"Rev, I just want to know what God has put me on earth to do. I'll do it; I just don't know what it is. How did you know what you were supposed to do? I mean, how did you decide to be a professor and preacher?"

"How do you know it is God talking to you and you ain't trippin'?"

These are the types of questions I get all the time from young adults. I often say to them, "You a trip, but God ain't trippin'. You trippin', but God ain't trippin'." One foundational thought drives what we do in young adult ministry: we are going to walk together and not trip out over what you are going through or dealing with. Young adults are in a period of reexamining their lives, motives, call, convictions, and theology. Young adults come to the ministry looking for a safe place where they can wrestle with developing answers to big questions. These big questions aren't asked in passing. The questions they ask are at the heart of what young adult ministry is all about, questions of identity and purpose. I can't count the times I've had conversation with young adults about hearing the voice of God and discerning their call and purpose against the backdrop of a life they haven't quite put together yet.

The driving force behind their quest is linked to their understanding of what they have been divinely designed to do. They want to be used by God and to use their gifts to glorify God. Young adults are looking for a way to know beyond a shadow of a doubt what God has called them to do and be. I find in these conversations that they are drawn to my story. My story looks linear to them; they think my call was clear early in my life and I just followed some plan. When I actually unpack my story for them, I expose the twists and turns involved in understanding what a person is to do and be. In the process of sharing with them, I can sense their relief. They realize that their struggle isn't unique to them; they realize that I and their peers had and have similar struggles. It is these struggles of identity, purpose, and divine direction that lie at the heart of young adult ministry.

What Are the Real Issues?

At the root of ministry with and to young adults is what I like to call the "great quest," the question of purpose. The great quest is tied up with the great question: What have I been put on earth to be and do? This is both an identity question and a spiritual question. This question has theological and sociological implications. Young adults are in the process of defining themselves apart from their parents and in relationship to their peers. They are stretching out on their quest for a new life interdependent with their parents. There is a tension between what their parents defined for them and what they now have to define for themselves. They look back at their parents and upbringing and ask, "Do I want to go back to what I know or move ahead to what I don't know?" If I move ahead, I will need to find a way to structure and define this future thing. The biblical foundation for quest, purpose, success, and significance is that famous Pauline passage of Ephesians 2:8-10 as Paul invites the readers to struggle with their divine design and purpose as outlined by God: "For it is by grace you have been saved, through faith—and this not from yourselves, it is the gift of God—not by works, so that no one can boast. For we are God's workmanship, created in Christ Jesus to do good works, which God prepared in advance for us to do" (NIV).

The Ephesians 2:8-10 Quest Question

What has God designed young adults to be and do? What are those works that God has prepared for them? Sharon Parks makes the quest question clear in her book *Big Questions, Worthy Dreams* as she characterizes the questions young adults are asking. Parks says, "These are questions of meaning, purpose, and faith; they are asked not just on the immediate horizon of where we spend the night. In young adulthood, as we step beyond the home that has sheltered us and look into the night sky, we can begin in a more conscious way to ask the ancient questions: Who am I under these stars? Does my life have a place and a purpose? Are we—am I—alone?"[1] Young adults come to the church with these questions of meaning on their hearts. Young adult ministry must have at its root the mission of helping them find answers as their faith in God, themselves, and the community of faith is developed. It means bringing them into a community of faith that recognizes and honors the developmental work they are doing and walks with them. The church has to be that place of under-standing and support as this intense construction and reconstruc-tion takes place in their lives.

The young adult developmental period feels like life and death for those experiencing it. It is a valley experience as they seek what's next (the immediate) and what tomorrow has in store for them (the future). Young adults are doing serious life work, and the church has to have an intentional ministry effort that pays attention to this work they are doing and helps them through it. Many young adults leave the church during this period, and as a result they are trying to do this developmental work in the context of popular culture, which bombards them with mixed messages. In the church they need to hear a message that engages the messages they are getting from the culture while teaching them ways to seek counsel from God, godly friends, and leaders as they walk through this important phase of life.

Alexandra Robbins and Abby Wilner, the authors of the book, *Quarterlife Crisis*, describe this period of life as the "quarterlife crisis." Robins and Wilner compare the quarterlife crisis (between the late teens and early twenties) to what is commonly referred to and accepted in the culture as the midlife crisis. They say:

> While the midlife crisis revolves around a doomed sense of stagnancy, of a life set on pause while the rest of the world rattles on, the quarterlife crisis is a response to overwhelming instability, constant change, too many choices, and panicked sense of helplessness....The resulting overwhelming senses of helplessness and cluelessness, of indecision and apprehension, make up the real common experience we call the quarterlife crisis.... Twentysomethings believe they are alone and that they are having a much more difficult transition period than their peers—because the twenties are supposed to be "easy," because no one talks about these problems, and because the difficulties are therefore so unexpected.[2]

Because no one talks about or recognizes the quarterlife crisis, the young adults' experiences that feel like life and death go unnoticed by the larger culture, especially in church culture. As a result, they are left shivering, alone, afraid, and confused, waiting for someone to stop by their house and talk with them as they walk along this lonely way. In the Bible we see Jesus both recognizing and responding to quarterlife crisis.

Jesus' Ministry: A Model of Response

Ministry to young adults was a significant part of Jesus' ministry during his time on earth. We know that many of the disciples were young men searching for meaning, identity, and life purpose. We can of course assume that many of the women who where part of Jesus' crowd were also young adults searching for the answer to the big questions of life. We know, for example, that Mary and Martha were close to Jesus and supportive of his ministry. Their search for an answer to what is most important in life is recorded in Luke 10:38-42. Mary and Martha are doing the work of young adults as they ask big questions and listen to Jesus' answers. In essence Martha asks, "Do I do what is expected of me, or do I do what excites me? Do I sit and listen, or do I stay busy? How do I find God and find out what God wants of me?" The Mary and Martha story exposes some of the tension experienced in the lives of young adults:

> As Jesus and his disciples were on their way, he came to a village where a woman named Martha opened her home to him. She had a sister called Mary, who sat at the Lord's feet listening to what he said. But Martha was distracted by all the preparations that had to be made. She came to him and asked, "Lord, don't you care that my sister has left me to do the work by myself? Tell her to help me!"

"Martha, Martha," the Lord answered, "you are worried and upset about many things, but only one thing is needed. Mary has chosen what is better, and it will not be taken away from her." (Luke 10:38-42 NIV)

Interpreting this passage for young adults today, we see on the one hand that they are trying to stay busy. They are trying out school, majors, jobs, and all sorts of hobbies, seeking to find what satisfies them. This is what Robbins and Wilner call the "trial-and-error method." "A lot of twentysomethings at least have some similarly vague idea of what they want to do with their lives, whether it is a job, a hobby, or a lifestyle. Then they use the trial-and-error method to find the precise fit for their strengths and tastes."[3] The trial-and-error model is typical of young adult development, and it must be encouraged as young adults try to find their way. Martha was in the middle of the trial-and-error crises. She was busy doing things, but she wasn't taking time to hear from God as she worked out what was next.

When Martha complained about Mary, Jesus was clear that Mary had made the better choice by choosing to sit and commune with him. Many young adults are busy running around trying to find out what God wants, what they want, and what the world wants on a trial-and-error basis while there isn't a place for them to sit. A key theological theme in young adult ministry must be making a place for young adults to sit and listen to God. They want and need a place to reflect on God's words and ways. They need a break from the busy, a place where their resting and sitting at the feet of Jesus is appreciated and they are not criticized for what appears to be doing nothing. This *is* doing something, and they must be encouraged to spend time listening to God.

We find in the Gospels that Jesus is always making a time for people to sit together and talk about life questions. Likewise, today's young adults must be allowed to sit down together with

God and those God has put in place to love them as they search for that God *thang*, or call, that is bigger than they are. Actually, in Scripture, a call is not something one looks for; it is something that comes to a person as he or she walks along the way and listens for God. When Jesus called the disciples into being what they were divinely designed to be, they weren't out looking—they were working and willing to hear what God had next for them.

Many young adults are caught between making a living, finishing a major, and doing what they really want to do—which in many cases they don't even know yet. It is unfair to ask twenty-year-olds what they want to do for the rest of their lives. They don't know. Neither did I when I was twenty. The culture insists they pick a college major and career path at eighteen or twenty, and many of them don't have a clue. They walk into something that they may eventually struggle with and fight to walk away from. In Mark's Gospel we see the calling of the first disciples as an example of the tension between doing what it takes just to get by and doing what God wants them to do:

> As Jesus walked beside the Sea of Galilee, he saw Simon and his brother Andrew casting a net into the lake, for they were fishermen. "Come, follow me," Jesus said, "and I will make you fishers of men." At once they left their nets and followed him.
> When he had gone a little farther, he saw James son of Zebedee and his brother John in a boat, preparing their nets. Without delay he called them, and they left their father Zebedee in the boat with the hired men and followed him. (Mark 1:16-20 NIV)

A lot can be inferred from this passage in regard to young adult ministry. Here we find young men engaged in doing work that is feeding them and those they love, but what they are doing to make ends meet isn't feeding their souls. They are looking for something. We know this to be true based on their response to Jesus' appeal to a life calling. In essence he asks them, "Do you want to do something other than be fishermen?" He offers them an opportunity to do something bigger than themselves, to change the world by being fishers of men and women instead of fish. Jesus is saying, "Come and find yourself and your call by following me, for I have come to change the world."

The response of Simon and Andrew was immediate. As the story proceeds, we see Jesus' call to James and John, and they, too, respond affirmatively and without delay. These brothers were probably close in age. They were also probably close in age to Jesus. These were young men, just like Mary and Martha were young women, and they were searching.

When Jesus extended these calls to follow him, he was in his late twenties or early thirties. The men and women he was calling to walk with him were young adults as well, and they had not gotten caught up in the religious hierarchy of their traditions. They had been raised around the synagogue, but they were open to hearing and being something different and new. They supported Jesus in his challenging of tradition, for they were at a point in their lives when they were open to new and fresh ideas.

Developmentally it all makes sense, because the early adult years are a time of questioning. It is a time of examining not only what one believes, but why. Young adults are deciding whether they want to be like their parents who are church members. Robbins and Wilner say: "One of the most challenging shifts between childhood and adulthood is the changing relationship with parents. The familial link never disappears, of course—your parents will always be your parents and you will always be their child. But in the days after graduation, a twentysomething slowly comes to realize that the playing field is leveled to a certain extent because there is no longer that 'me adult, you kid' separation."[4]

While this change in relationship brings freedom, it also brings responsibility. And along with that comes a period of questioning: Who I am, and how will I live out my relationship with God? Since I am no longer being dragged to church, will I go or not? If I go, what type of church will I go to?

Moving from Sunday School to Life

Young adults move from Sunday school into an intense period of reexamination and questioning. Some in this period tend to take extreme positions. There are religious zealots on the one hand and religious relativists or pragmatists on the other.[5] These extremes run deep in the phases of young adult development. Some young people may embrace a more radical faith than their parents and others may reject their parents' faith. Ministry with young adults provides space for the extremes and weaves them into a tapestry of intentional faith development that leads them to a place of contentment in Jesus Christ.

Jesus provided his early disciples with a mentoring type relationship. He walked with them and taught them by taking advantage of teaching moments from life experiences that were relevant, applicable, contextual, and life altering. These moments offered a new way of seeing the world and ministry. From the beginning he showed them that following and serving God make a real difference. As Jesus called his first disciples, he moved them right into ministry. No training process preceded their ministry. Ministry itself became training. Today's young adults want to learn on the go as well. They are not linear in their thinking and praxis. They are accustomed to multitasking and to multisensory activities. They answer e-mail while listening to music or watching TV, text message while talking, and search the Web while the professor is lecturing.

Multitasking and learning on the go are not necessarily new things. Jesus and the disciples were doing them two thousand years ago. Look, for example, at a twenty-four-hour period in the life of Jesus and his disciples from the book of Mark.

They went to Capernaum, and when the Sabbath came, Jesus went into the synagogue and began to teach. The people were amazed at his teaching, because he taught them as one who had authority, not as the teachers of the law. Just then a man in their synagogue who was possessed by an evil spirit cried out, "What do you want with us, Jesus of Nazareth? Have you come to destroy us? I know who you are—the Holy One of God!"

"Be quiet!" said Jesus sternly. "Come out of him!" The evil spirit shook the man violently and came out of him with a shriek.

The people were all so amazed that they asked each other, "What is this? A new teaching—and with authority! He even gives orders to evil spirits and they obey him." News about him spread quickly over the whole region of Galilee.

As soon as they left the synagogue, they went with James and John to the home of Simon and Andrew. Simon's mother-in-law was in bed with a fever, and they told Jesus about her. So he went to her, took her hand and helped her up. The fever left her and she began to wait on them.

That evening after sunset the people brought to Jesus all the sick and demon-possessed. The whole town gathered at the door, and Jesus healed many who had various diseases. He also drove out many demons, but he would not let the demons speak because they knew who he was.

Very early in the morning, while it was still dark, Jesus got up, left the house and went off to a solitary place, where he prayed. Simon and his companions went to look for him, and when they found him, they exclaimed: "Everyone is looking for you!"

Jesus replied, "Let us go somewhere else—to the nearby villages—so I can preach there also. That is why I have come." So he traveled throughout Galilee, preaching in their synagogues and driving out demons. (1:21-39 NIV)

After Jesus delivered the demon-possessed man in the synagogue, the people were amazed at Jesus' authority and wondering at his new kind of teaching. Can you imagine what his new disciples were saying? "This brother is for real. We are onto something here!" They saw Jesus' power and the promise of the ministry. It is as though right away Jesus felt the need to show them by word and deed that the ministry they had enlisted in was bigger than fishing. They went from fishing one day to being a part of a healing ministry the next.

Today's young adults want to be part of a ministry that helps heal them as they go through one of the roughest periods of their lives. They are struggling with everything from generational family stuff to their own sexual identity and relationship issues. This time of intense conflict and pain demands a ministry that calls out by name those things they are dealing with, puts those things on the table, and helps them get free. They are looking for new, exciting teaching of God's Word that gets in them and transforms them. This is what the disciples were a part of with Jesus. Young adult ministry needs to have the same sense of excitement, boldness, and drama to hold the attention and involvement of young adults.

Is This Church for Real?

Young adults are looking for confirmation that what they are doing is actually making a difference. They are not willing simply to come to church on Sunday and go through the motions. They question the relevance and power of the church. They critique form and fashion that don't lead to deliverance. If ministry does not make a difference in the world or in their lives, they are out of there. Jesus understood this. As soon as Jesus demonstrated the power of God in the deliverance of the demon-possessed man, he walked with his disciples to the home of Simon and Andrew. He was now about to show them how this ministry addressed their personal lives. Simon's mother-in-law was in bed with a fever, and Jesus healed her. Then many others brought those who were sick and demon-possessed, and Jesus healed them.

The key here is ministry that makes a difference. Jesus wasn't offering religious platitudes or promising to do something later for those who were hurting. He responded on the spot in a way that made a lasting difference. Young adults want to be involved in ministry that is real, tangible, and making a difference in the here and now. George Barna calls these types of young adults I am describing religious revolutionaries. He says, "[There is] a new breed of disciples of Jesus Christ. They are not willing to play religious games and aren't interested in being part of a religious community that is not intentionally and aggressively advancing God's kingdom. They are people who want more of God—much more—in their lives. And they are doing whatever it takes to get it."[6]

The disciples of Jesus got more of God; they were able to touch God, sit with God, and see God act. Young adults in the twenty-first century want this type of closeness with God. They want institutions to get out of the way and allow God access to God's people and help them get closer to God. They hate red tape. Jesus didn't have a wall between him and the people. He gave them access and the ability to get involved and start working with the ministry today.

A ministry that doesn't empower young adults to live an edited life in an unedited world with and among sin and sinners will not meet their needs. They need to be empowered to sit the way Jesus sat with tax collectors and sinners. This is the type of faith praxis that makes sense to both zealots and relativists. Zealots have decided that a turn away from the world is the answer, so they reject and condemn the entire "worldly" project. While this rejection brings an initial sense of security and rightness, if they are to develop a mature faith, they will have to question that rigid approach. A ministry that pulls them "out of the world" will not help them grow in their faith or ability to deal with the contradictions in their approach. Their approach contains contradictions, because it is impossible for them to completely withdraw from the world when they work in the world, drive in the world, go to school in the world, listen to the world's radio and television, use the world's Internet, wear the world's clothes, and use the world's cell phones. It is impossible for them not to be in the world. They have to be empowered with ways to live in the world but not be just like that world they live in. This empowerment requires an encounter with God's Word that reveals God's ways and methods for living in the world they can't leave.

Growing Up in the Church and Leaving:
"Will I Come Back?"
by Nastasia and Nicole Watkins

Nastasia and Nicole Watkins were raised in church. Their father is a pastor, and their mother has been a youth director. Once they enrolled in college at North Carolina A & T State University, they found themselves not going to church. Here they tell their story and the story of many of their friends who were raised in church but aren't going while they are in college.

Nastasia Watkins During my growing-up years, every Sunday, Monday, and Wednesday was a day at the church—the early service and Sunday school on Sunday, choir practice on Monday, and

Bible study on Wednesday. After eighteen years of the same routine, it became redundant, and I came to believe that I knew every story in the Bible. For many eighteen-year-olds, the next step after high school is college. Most of my friends went to college, and many of them, like me, were tired of church. College, to me, meant freedom—freedom from rules, parents, curfews, and consequently, church. I began to question my reason for attending church without the usual pressure from my parents. I refused to be one of those unhappy children who well into adulthood do everything that is expected of them simply out of habit. College seemed to be the right place for my enlightenment about religion, relationships, and my future. I had the freedom to think for myself and decide for myself, and that is what I did.

I met many new people with views different than mine, and I began to feel no connection to the beliefs of most Christians on campus. As an outspoken liberal student at a historically black university, I felt as though my views and beliefs about the government did not coincide with Christian teachings. Members of the Christian group on campus, Youth Taking Charge, questioned my preference to wear high heels to class, attend church sporadically, and swear on occasion. Their judgmental attitudes drove me further away from the church. It appeared to me that many of my peers who professed to be Christians had lost touch with the true teachings of Jesus, and I did not want to be in their presence. According to them, my appearance and weekly attendance to a building they called church determined my level of faith in the Lord. I felt that not taking my Bible to class and not attempting to convert every person I came in contact with didn't make me less of a Christian than they were. My anger toward them and others caused me to become angry with the church. I refused to be labeled an ignorant Southern evangelical who believed anything spoken by someone with the letters *R-e-v* in front of his or her name. I was smarter than those people; I was educated; I questioned authority; and I was a liberal Christian who didn't attend church. This was my new identity in Christ, and it is still my identity today.

I don't know if I will go back to church. If I do, it will have to be a place that encourages me to think for myself. I want a church that engages in politics, empowers women, and helps people walk that thin line between the church and the world. Don't condemn me because I don't buy the whole line of your theological argument. Give me some room to be me. After all, when I went to college, I wanted room to be me. So for me church has to be a place that gives people space and doesn't condemn people for not being perfect. I may go back to church one day, but I have yet to find a church that understands the concerns I have and is willing to talk with me and people like me about these issues. If they had such a place for young adults during the week and worship services that spoke to my head and my heart, then maybe I would return.

Nicole Watkins While growing up, hitting the snooze button and missing church was not an option on any Sunday. My father was a preacher, and God was and is the head of my family's house. When coming to college in 2005, I thought it would be easy to find a "good" church home. However, being a freshman and not having a car made it hard to find a church within walking distance. There were three churches around my freshman dorm that I would force myself to attend. All three of the churches were "dead." There were very few young adults at the churches, and the members were not nice. It was if we were invisible. Where was that old Southern hospitality? I guess I was looking for some type of red carpet—or at least some greeters! This nonwelcoming attitude really surprised me. After all, I was at a historically black college, and these churches had to know we were there—weren't they expecting us? I thought I was going to find churches hunting us down and hugging us when we came, with people my age in every pew. When I found the opposite of what I expected, I was taken aback.

Disappointed and discouraged, I didn't give up the search for a place to call "my church." The churches my roommate and I visited were more of the same. We would go and sit and receive nothing. The sermons and music were so old and out of touch that it was like I was caught in the 1960s. Eventually my roommate and I got tired of attending churches that did not fulfill us spiritually like the churches we had grown up in back home. Even though they were the same denomination, we just felt so out of place. We heard about church van shuttles that came to the local student union to transport students to various churches. So one morning we arrived at the union at 8:30 a.m. and stayed until 9:30, but no church vans arrived. So much for that one. I was confounded. "What's the use?" I asked. I stopped searching and resorted to watching the occasional television ministry. I would go to church when I went home.

So from my freshmen year until now in my junior year, I have attended churches occasionally, especially when trying to pass a hard test (smile). Now I am a junior in college and have been blessed with a car. However, it has still been difficult for me to find a church home. I know that no church will be like the one back home, but I at least hoped to find churches with members who were inviting and smiled and made me feel welcome. I am still searching to find that church, and I am disappointed that I haven't found a church to call home yet.

QUESTIONS TO CONSIDER

1. To what degree is your church welcoming to young adults?

2. What has your church done to make sure it is welcoming to young adults?

3. How would your church deal with Peter?

4. How does the church deal with the Peter types who can be conflicted and confused while trying to be faithful?

5. What is unique about your city that would fight against young adults' faith journey?

6. How willing is your church to give permission for young adults to experiment and deal with the transitions they are experiencing?

7. How does your church walk alongside young adults as they go on their journey?

8. Why is it important for the church to walk gently regarding the issue of being in the world but not of the world?

9. When you were a young adult, how did you feel about the church?

10. Have you ever asked a group of young adults what they thought about your church? What were their responses?

NOTES

1. Sharon Daloz Parks, *Big Questions, Worthy Dreams: Mentoring Young Adults in Their Search for Meaning, Purpose, and Faith* (San Francisco: Jossey-Bass, 2000), 35.

2. Alexandra Robbins and Abby Wilner, *Quarterlife Crisis: The Unique Challenges of Life in Your Twenties* (New York: Penguin Putnam, 2001), 4–5.

3. Ibid., 31.

4. Ibid., 55.

5. H. S. Vigeveno, *13 Men Who Changed the World* (Ventura, CA: Regal, 1986), 21, 55.

6. George Barna, *Revolution* (Wheaton, IL: Tyndale, 2005), 7.

6

Preaching to and Teaching Young Adults: Crafting a Word to Be Heard

After the Mark 1 account we read in chapter 5 where Jesus was teaching and healing in the Capernaum synagogue and then withdrew to some nearby Galilean villages to minister, he again entered Capernaum, and the people heard that he had come home.

So many people gathered that there was no room left, not even outside the door, and he preached the Word to them. Some men came, bringing to him a paralytic, carried by four of them. Since they could not get him to Jesus because of the crowd, they made an opening in the roof above Jesus and, after digging through it, lowered the mat the paralyzed man was lying on. When Jesus saw their faith, he said to the paralytic, "Son, your sins are forgiven."

Now some teachers of the law were sitting there, thinking to themselves, "Why does this fellow talk like that? He's blaspheming! Who can forgive sins but God alone?"

Immediately Jesus knew in his spirit that this was what they were thinking in their hearts, and he said to them, "Why are you thinking these things? Which is easier: to say to the paralytic, 'Your sins are forgiven,' or to say, 'Get up, take your mat and walk'? But that you may know that the Son of Man has authority on earth to forgive sins..." He said to the paralytic, "I tell you, get up, take your mat and go home." He got up, took his mat and walked out in full view of them all. This amazed everyone and they praised God, saying, "We have never seen anything like this!"

Once again Jesus went out beside the lake. A large crowd came to him, and he began to teach them. As he walked along, he saw Levi son of Alphaeus sitting at the tax collector's booth. "Follow me," Jesus told him, and Levi got up and followed him.

While Jesus was having dinner at Levi's house, many tax collectors and "sinners" were eating with him and his disciples, for there were many who followed him. When the teachers of the law who were Pharisees saw him eating with the "sinners" and tax collectors, they asked his disciples: "Why does he eat with tax collectors and 'sinners'?"

On hearing this, Jesus said to them, "It is not the healthy who need a doctor, but the sick. I have not come to call the righteous, but sinners" (Mark 2:1-17 NIV).

Effective teaching and preaching with young adults occurs best when it is contextualized. Teaching young adults has to be contextual, with living-world examples that touch where they itch and where they hurt. Jesus taught his disciples in the moment by being sensitive to their context. He didn't take them out of the world to teach them, but taught them about their faith while in the world. There were moments of reflection and isolation in Jesus' ministry with his disciples, but those moments of retreat were just that—retreat. Jesus' teaching model was active; the teaching happened in the process of doing. Young adults want to engage the world they are living in. A phrase we use at First AME Church in Los Angeles is "We are about teaching young adults to live an edited life in an unedited world while being in touch with the Word, the world, on point and uncut!" How did Jesus do it? Jesus engaged the very things and people that the religious leaders of the day had either condemned or had nothing to do with. We see this in Jesus' calling of his next disciple, Levi.

Levi, also known as Matthew, was the lowest of the low, a tax collector, but Jesus called him to be a disciple. He didn't call the religious leaders of the day; he called a tax collector, a sinner. At first this appears almost contradictory, but upon further reflection, we see how this fits with Jesus' model of ministry to young adults. Young adults are going through a period of life when they are hanging out with their friends. They are not at youth group; they are at the club, sitting in a friend's dorm room, visiting someone's apartment, or riding in a car full of friends. These friends may or may not be Christians, but in the mix of young adult life, they are trying things out, making new friends, and pondering the possibility of picking up new habits. Jesus not only called Levi, but he also hung out with Levi's friends, eating and drinking. The religious leaders were taken aback. Nevertheless, this is the very model of ministry that worked with the young adults Jesus was trying to reach and bring into the church.

What can we learn from the Levi story as it relates to young adult ministry? When Jesus first saw Levi, he was sitting at the tax collector's booth hanging out with the "wrong" people. Jesus didn't call him out of that life or tell him to stop associating with that crowd. Instead, Jesus dined at Levi's house with the tax collector and his friends. Levi accepted the call to follow Jesus, but instead of leaving after the call and sequestering himself, he followed Jesus back into the uncut, unedited world of tax collectors. They sat and had dinner, wine, and a fine time together. Interestingly, when the Pharisees saw this, they were appalled and began to critique Jesus. But the young disciples found this challenge of tradition affirming and uplifting. They engaged in the meal and conversation as Jesus modeled for them what he would later teach and pray in John 17:15: "My prayer is not that you take them out of the world but that you protect them from the evil one" (NIV). Jesus didn't call them out of the world; he led them into the world.

The Wow Factor

When Jesus taught, the people were amazed by his delivery and his content. Jesus knew the culture and used it as his background as he talked to people. He didn't use the culture as a whipping post or a poster child for what was wrong with people, but instead used it as a platform to talk to the people about the things of God. If you are going to reach young adults with the Word of God, then the model Jesus uses in his ministry is a perfect example of what works. In no way does Jesus water down what God requires, but he does present the truth in such a way that it can be heard by his audience, and when it is heard the Word will do its liberating work.

Young adults have been raised on hip-hop. Whether we like or appreciate hip-hop is not an argument we want to get into at this point. The point we want to make is that they have heard a word crafted by some of the most gifted wordsmiths alive. To hear a story told in rhyme and rhythm is awesome. When young adults sit in the pew or at Bible study, they need a word that is engaging while speaking through and to the culture and that moves them to respond intellectually, emotionally, psychologically, and spiritually.

Real-World Preaching and Teaching

Young adults come to church after watching a "real" world on television that isn't real but rather surreal—television shows like *Real World, College Hill, A Shot at Love with Tila Tequila, Bad Girls, The Hills, Runs House, Flava of Love, American Idol, Making the Band, America's Next Top Model.* All of the shows are shot over weeks and condensed into a thirty-minute or one-hour format, and young adults think they are watching what "really happens." Editing and scripting appear to be absent from the presentation. The fact that young adults think that they are watching life unfold in front of them, unlike sitcoms or television dramas that they know are scripted TV shows, presents an interesting dilemma for today's preachers and teachers. How do we teach about the real world when the world of make-believe (i.e., reality television) has become the "real." Where is the line between real and fiction?

The word young adults have to hear must engage the reality television world and hip-hop by bringing them back to reality. This means a word that will be heard is a word that is presented in a real-world context, is story-based, intriguing, and gripping, and deals with truth. Young adults are searching for truth and realness in the shows they watch and the music they listen to. Preachers and teachers have the job of revealing how unreal these shows are while offering the truth as a way of confronting the lie (John 8:32). This truth should be presented with the fiction and real worlds in view. As hip-hop is conversant with the larger culture, preaching and teaching with young adults must be done in conversation with the world they watch.

Take Them Seriously: Push Them to the Prophetic

As we talk about preaching truth to young adults in the context of the real, we must emphasize that young adults must be challenged to change the world. Bakari Kitwana has said that the hip-hop generation is activist-minded but not activist.[1] If Kitwana is right—and I believe he is—this pushes the African American church to introduce young adults to the prophetic preaching tradition that will empower them to change the world. According to Marvin A. McMickle, author of the book, *Where Have All the Prophets Gone?*, "Prophetic preaching shifts the focus of a congregation from what is happening to them as a local church to what is happening to them as a part of society. Prophetic preaching then asks the question, 'What is the role or appropriate response of our congregation…?' Prophetic preaching points out those false gods of comfort."[2] A shift has to occur from the desire for wealth and fame to social change. Young adults must see that their faith is not another party—that is, praise party—but rather that their faith is about personal salvation and social responsibility as well.

When you look at the religious landscape in the African American community, the churches that are preaching praise and wealth are attracting people, but there is something missing in this message. As the prophetic has been replaced by praise party, the balance has been lost. African Americans have always known how to praise God, and we should never lose that gift. But we must maintain our tradition of fighting for social change as well. The African American church has embraced Psalm 150 and Matthew 25:31-46. McMickle points out that an overemphasis on praise that isn't held in tension with social responsibility is dangerous. He says, "There is a constant call to 'praise God' that is seldom, if ever followed up with a challenge to serve God in tangible ways that are of benefit to our brothers and sisters, to our neighbors and friends, or to the widows, orphans, and strangers who are constantly referenced to in the Bible."[3] I hear Amos saying, "Take away from Me the noise of your songs, for I will not hear the melody of your stringed instruments. But let justice run down like water, And righteousness like a mighty stream" (Amos 5:23-24).

Young adults must be confronted with a word that moves them from praising to protesting. They are inheriting an African American community that is in trouble from poverty to HIV-AIDS, to lack of health care, to underfunded schools—the list goes on. As Robert Michael Franklin has proclaimed in his book *Crisis in the Village*, we must do something to get the village back together.[4] A preached word that doesn't call young adults to accountability and social responsibility is an empty word. They want to hear truth that sets them and their people free.

> "The Spirit of the LORD is upon Me,
> Because He has anointed Me
> To preach the gospel to the poor;
> He has sent Me to heal the brokenhearted,
> To proclaim liberty to the captives
> And recovery of sight to the blind,
> To set at liberty those who are oppressed." (Luke 4:18)

From Preacher to Preacher:
"What You Talkin' 'bout Reverend?"
by Kurtley Knight

Kurtley Knight is twenty-five years old. He is a graduate of Oakwood College in Huntsville, Alabama, where he received a Bachelor of Arts degree in ministerial theology. He is currently working to complete a Master of Divinity degree at Andrews University in Berrien Springs, Michigan.

Let's be honest: preaching to this generation of young adults is not only challenging; sometimes it can almost seem overwhelming. Yet week after week we preachers are called upon by God to mount the sacred desk and deliver his Word to the people, including young adults. Before we begin our weekly preaching preparation, however, we must stop and do some reflection on the cultural needs of young adults if we intend to be effective. As a preacher who is also a young adult, my experiences have lead me to practice three primary principles that leave young adults hungry for next week's message.

First, *"I'm hungry; stop feeding me milk."* In 1 Corinthians 3:2 Paul says, "I gave you milk, not solid food, for you were not yet ready for it" (NIV). Talking to the church at Corinth, Paul simply explains that though some of his hearers were adults, they were not ready for a steady diet of "solid" spiritual food. However, most young adults who attend our churches today are spiritually mature enough for "solid" spiritual food and not merely milk. Many of the issues they face require them to have a deeper understanding of God than is currently being presented by the church.

I learned this lesson the hard way one Sabbath morning during a sermon I preached while serving as an associate pastor in Los Angeles. I vividly remember this day, because a set of young adult twins who had been AWOL for months were in attendance. Unfortunately, I wasn't ready. I had wasted away the week, not giving adequate time to sermon preparation. Deciding to throw something together at the last minute, I hoped that my charisma would carry me (you know, you've been there before). The sermon was flat. I substituted style for content and paid the price. Afterward at the church potluck I had an opportunity to speak to the twins. After some small talk, I asked how they liked the morning sermon. Laughing, one of them responded, "You call that a sermon?" Amazed by the honesty, I swiftly replied, "What?" The other weighed in with a long discourse on why they had stopped coming to church. By the end of the conversation, they both agreed, "You gave us milk when we were hungry." My mouth literally dropped as I stood there knowing that not only had I been ineffective, but I also had failed in what God had called me to do: feed his flock.

Make no mistake: we as young adults want deep biblical and theological preaching that is hopeful, inspirational, and relational. We may be young, but we are adults who are capable of reading, processing, and thinking analytically. We are college graduates, graduate students, professionals, computer specialists, photographers, musicians, cosmetologists, physical therapists, tellers, cashiers, and entrepreneurs. When preaching isn't the "solid" spiritual food that we crave, it is a disservice both to God's Word and to us. Every time I "climb into the desk," I make it my goal never to let content suffer for the sake of charisma, for like starved children who haven't had food all day, young adults cry out, "Feed us."

The second principle is *"Show me what's around me."* The importance of postmodernism in regard to the way we preach cannot be overstated. We live in a postmodern culture that seeps into various areas of life. From the box office to the church office, the philosophy of postmodernism that thrives on the denunciation of absolute truth, the rejection of metanarratives (such as the concept of salvation history), and the embracing of relative truth influences countless people throughout the nation. This distinction is important because the contemporary preacher must be able to unveil for his or her listener from within the culture itself where cultural ideas are influencing our lives. Simply put, our preaching must be relevant.

I experienced this principle as I stood to preach to a young adult church in Indiana this past summer. Basing my sermon on Psalms 130, I attempted to discuss how God reveals himself in the deep places of our lives if only we are patient enough to wait. I began the sermon with an effective illustration I had seen on a Visa Check Card commercial. In every Visa Check Card commercial, using cash slows down the customers. In fact, what the commercial teaches its viewers is a very important spiritual lesson: if we as consumers are ever forced to wait, our lives turn into chaos. I carried this theme from those introductory comments to show how this impatience that the culture promotes deeply affects our spirituality. By the end of the intro and the transition into the body, I had my young adults hooked. Afterward, countless people told me that not only were they blessed, but they could also now see clearly the effects of the culture in their lives.

Young adults want to hear sermons that are relevant to the wider cultural situation. We desire to hear sermons that meet us where we are as we struggle with purpose, identity, and an uncertain future. Sermons about prosperity and sowing seed and obtaining material things from God do not whet the appetite of most young adults. Rather, sermons that help us think through how God would have us live in a non-Christian society pay greater dividends.

The third principle is *"Practice what you preach."* Once while preaching for a student-led campus revival at Oakwood College in Huntsville, Alabama, I experienced the importance of this principle. That weekend I spoke passionately about how much we hurt ourselves when we reject God's call on our lives, as illustrated in the words of Jesus to Paul in Acts 26:14, "It is hard for you to kick against the goads" (NIV). The sermon was specifically crafted for young adult hearers. In no way was this a shallow sermon. I spent hours in exegetical preparation, making sure I gave them a three-course meal and not milk. While shaking hands at the door, a young man whom I had met previously on campus remarked as he pulled me to the side, "I've watched you during our time here at Oakwood. You really touched me today." "How?" I asked. He responded, "What I saw today is how I see you trying to live your life. You were transparent, and I really appreciated that."

We as young adults are not concerned simply with biblical data, charismatic personality, or denominational liturgy. Instead, we are drawn to authentically spiritual people. Just as a hound dog can sniff out the single scent of an escapee from jail among all the various scents in the wet and muddy marshlands, so also can we distinguish if a preacher is truly a spiritual leader or if one's motivation is self-promotion. Probably the most important thing preachers can do to reach my peers is to live a life of spiritual authenticity.

In conclusion, some people place big significance on what style works best when preaching to young adults. It's my opinion that style is not so important. Take it from me: I am a manuscript preacher, which many would say does not work with young adults, but it has. If you do the same no matter what style you use, whether it be extemporaneous or manuscript, you can still be effective. Remember, they want "solid" food, cultural relevance, and an authentically lived spirituality. At least that's what they tell me!

QUESTIONS TO CONSIDER

To what extent do you have young adults in mind as you prepare and deliver your messages? Ask yourself the following questions as you consider the messages you prepare.

1. How do young adults hear?

2. How will I reach them with this message?

3. What will they be listening for in this message?

4. How can examples from popular culture be woven into this word to make it something they can relate to?

5. Why should young adults want to hear what I have to say?

6. What is on the minds of young adults as they come to worship or Bible study?

7. How real and raw is this word? What do I need to change to keep it real?

8. What real life issues am I focusing on in this word that relate to what young adults are dealing with?

9. How faithfully does this message engage the text? Have I done my exegetical homework?

10. Is this message substantive or superficial?

NOTES

1. Bakari Kitwana, *The Hip Hop Generation: Young Blacks and the Crisis in African American Culture* (New York: Basic Civitas Books, 2003), 154.

2. Marvin A. McMickle, *Where Have All The Prophets Gone? Reclaiming Prophetic Preaching in America* (Cleveland, OH: Pilgrim, 2006), 2.

3. Ibid., 79.

4. Robert Michael Franklin, *Crisis in the Village: Restoring Hope in African American Communities* (Minneapolis: Fortress, 2007).

7

The New Deal in the New Church: The Future of the Church Is in Its Young Adults

Then Joshua commanded the officers of the people saying, "Pass through the camp and command the people, saying, 'Prepare provisions for yourselves, for within three days you will cross over this Jordan, to go in to possess the land which the LORD your God is giving you to possess.'"
JOSHUA 1:10-11

The young adult leaders of the church will be your Joshuas. They don't wait; they don't procrastinate; they want things now, and they are willing to go get them. The preceding generation was a patient generation; we marched, we voted, we protested. But this generation has been raised ordering fast food from the drive-thru window, using high-speed Internet service, and watching satellite television. They can demand a show when they want to see it. No more going to get a DVD or a VHS tape; they can download a movie, watch a television program on their iPod, or set their TiVo to record so they can watch at their convenience. This is a new way of doing things that calls for a new leadership style that will shift how we do church in the African American community. The shift from Moses to Joshua is a biblical model that highlights the difference between the baby boomer generation and the hip-hop generation. "This generation, itself, wants to be in charge."[1] They come in the door ready to lead a new way in a new direction, based on their socialization in a right-now generation that has been waiting too long. How do we equip them to lead while integrating them into the leadership ranks of the church?

In their heart, mind, and eyes, the hip-hop generation feels that the former generation held on too long. Bakari Kitwana is clear on this issue in *The Hip Hop Generation*: the former generation held on too long and has yet to pass the reins to the hip-hop generation.[2] The hip-hop generation feels as if the old ways of doing things have had their day, and it is now time for a new way to deal with the complexities of living in a technological world. Change has to occur if the church is going to serve the present age effectively. This calls for a new way of leading. When you look at Joshua and Moses, the differences are obvious. When I read and discussed this biblical story with a group of young adults, they were amazed that Moses didn't resign and turn the reins over to Joshua. I wonder if Moses should have resigned after the first ten years of walking in the wilderness. How long should we make Joshua wait?

A New Way of Doing Things: Relevant, Real, Relational, Transforming

The new way of doing things for young adults is founded on their ability to multitask. They are accustomed to doing while planning and planning while doing. Their approach to life is event-based and relevance-driven. The esoteric, philosophical approach is one thing, but theirs is a hands-on approach that gets them involved and moves them to act. They don't serve out of duty; they serve to make a difference. Gone are the days of "This is my church no matter what." Today, for young adults, their church can be a group of friends, their immediate family, or the new soon-to-be megachurch down the street. Denominational loyalty is a thing of the past. They have been raised in an age when the churches that have attracted them have worn their denominational labels low. The persona of the pastor is connected to the church that has attracted them. They want a church that ministers to their needs, involves them, and embraces updated ways of doing things—and *that* church becomes their church.

The new way of doing things is centered on needs-based ministry approaches that are relevant, real, and life transforming. Being involved in denominational meetings that build relationships but aren't productive will not work with young adults. They want to lead and be involved to make a lasting difference in their lives and in the life of the church and community. Going to denominational meetings that appear to have an internal focus is not their idea of leadership. Fighting for a post on the board of the national body and paying dues, assessments, or conference claims will not excite young adults. They want to be actively engaged in what they see as meaningful ministry, and they want to see their dollars make a tangible difference in the lives of others—especially their local church. They want to touch and be touched as they lead to make a difference.

New Ministry Leaders—A Changing of the Guard: Relational Leaders in Relationship with Others

Young adults are yearning to lead in the context of face-to-face relationships and via appropriate uses of technology. Rather than making communication less personal, the use of technology actually draws people together. From instant messaging to texting, to e-mailing, to the use of the cell phone to call right away from anywhere, young adults are accustomed to being instantly in touch.

They want to lead in an environment where they can feel connected via the sources with which they are used to being connected. Nevertheless, their desire and need for face-to-face communication is not diminished. The use of technology enhances face-to-face communication, as they can be in touch all day every day with those they are in leadership with. This expectation of being in relationship as they lead is critical for their success.

In the context of the church, even in mega-ministries, young adults want to feel connected to their pastor. This connection can be facilitated via preaching, podcasting, e-letters, or video streaming. They are also looking for integrity in their leaders. Their brokenness in terms of familial relationships follows them to the church. It is important for pastors and their families to serve as models for young adults who are looking up to them for something they may never have had. They aren't looking for a perfect model, but they do want an honest model. They see their pastor as a major part of their relationship with God. Therefore it is vital to find ways to reach out to them as often as possible by a variety of means. To put it simply, they want to hear from the church and to feel connected as family in both the small and large church.

Young Families: This Is How We Do It

The young African American family is a unique configuration in the eyes of baby boomers. The stereotypical family of a mother, father, and 2.5 children is not the reality for today's young adults. It is not unusual to have babies out of wedlock. The terms "my baby daddy" or "my baby mamma" are common. These terms refer to the fact that there is no longer a relational connection between the parents of the child; their connection is only to the baby they conceived. This kind of brokenness is common among young adults. "Father absence (men who have not seen their children during the past year or more) in poor communities is approximately 40 percent, and nonmarital birthrate in African American communities hovers around 70 percent."[3] As the numbers of children born to single parents rise, the question for the church is how to deal with the crisis. These children will be the leaders of the church of the future, so the intentionality of developing young adult leaders in a family atmosphere is critical.

It is also vital that a young adult pastor or a senior pastor shepherd young families in the church in a family atmosphere. Something as simple as having a weekly or regularly scheduled meal to sit and talk with young adults is important. At FAME I am convinced that the success of our young adult ministry was more about our sit-down dinners after Bible study than it was the Bible study and the various ministries. The young adults wanted the young adult pastor's time and attention. As one who was not in their peer group, I became like a father mentor to them. My wife, Vanessa, and I served them in love, and they wanted to touch both of us. The young adult ministry became a family. The question we had to confront was how the young adults were going to get from the young adult table (like the children's table at Thanksgiving) to the adult table. We have to grow them up in the family and move them from the table to the kitchen. They are ready to prepare the food—or are they? If they are not ready, we must make them ready to lead by developing them in the family.

The Future of the African American Church

The future of the African American church is in the hands of our young adults who were raised on hip-hop. "Without question, the greatest potential of the Black Church today resides in the group we call 'young adults.'"[4] It is up to the church to take the responsibility to evangelize them, bring them into the church, and learn from them, while simultaneously growing them into mature Christians who have a respect for tradition. This respect for tradition is critical, but at the same time, it can't be used in such a way as to block the new things that young adults will bring to the church. Tradition must be used as a history lesson. Young adults should be informed about the history of the local church, the African American church at large, and their denominational affiliation. Young adults' disdain or disrespect for tradition is misunderstood, because it most cases it is simply a lack of knowledge and a disconnectedness from the past.

The connection of the old and the new is essential. Young adults must understand what they are building on. Paul put it best when he said, "Each one should be careful how he builds" (1 Corinthians 3:10 NIV). Young adults must understand that they are building on a firm foundation. The African American church in all of its glory isn't a new thing. When W. E. B. DuBois walked into Bethel African Methodist Episcopal Church in 1899 when he was doing research for his classic text *The Philadelphia Negro*, he saw the first megachurch. It was DuBois who later extolled the beauty, majesty, and power of the African American church. From the works of Benjamin Mays, C. Eric Lincoln, Lawrence Mamiya, Albert Rabetou, Kelly Brown Douglas, and so many other scholars, the legacy of the richness of the African American church has been chronicled. Young adults must know that history of the African American church as the center of the community and as an agent of liberation and reconciliation. In an age of brokenness, the church cannot be recreated into a praise center that isn't a part of the prophetic tradition of the African American church. Knowing and respecting the history of the church will help guide our young adults to lead in new directions while being guided by the past.

Young adults are having a mixed relationship with the African American church largely due to the lack of dialogue between the old and the new. As new types of African American churches are emerging, there is a disconnect from the heart of what the African American church has been to the African American community. As much as young adults are looking for something new, the baby must not be thrown out with the bath water. Young adults still want deep relationships with their elders. They want to sit at the welcome table for a meal. They want people to know their names. They want a hug and a word of encouragement. They want to know that God loves them and that the church loves them and welcomes them. They want good preaching and good singing. As much as things change, much remains the same. Simply put, the African American church simply needs to be what it has always been—the African American church!

"There Is No Room in the Church": A Young Adult Couple with Children in and out of Church
by Ronnie and Tiffany Maxwell

Ronnie and Tiffany Maxwell are two young professionals, married with three young children. They talk about their search for a church home and what they were looking for, what they found, and what they didn't find in their quest.

Ronnie Maxwell Roughly one and a half years ago, I ended my relationship with attending church. The relationship between me and the megachurch lasted for more than six years. The following are some things that attracted me to the church: young pastor, pastor married with children, promotion of prosperity and men taking leadership, promotion of the importance of marriage and the family, practical yet biblically based teaching.

During this six-year relationship, I developed a belief that if I prayed, gave, and had faith, all things were possible—or in the words of Kanye West, I would have "the good life." But during this time I went through many changes in my life and realized that I was missing the mark. I started to follow the man of God and not God. I was caught in the mission and vision of the pastor and lost focus of the mission and vision for my life. In the process I never learned who God was for me. During my courtship with the megachurch, I stopped being me, because I was made to feel like I was sinning if I cursed, drank alcohol, listened to rap, hip-hop, or R&B music, or went out to a club. The church attempted to put all people in a box, by which I mean they taught that if you were a true Christian, you wouldn't do any of the things listed above.

I'm me....I'm me....I'm me....Who you?...You not me.
—Lil Wayne

I would always hear the saying "We are in the world but not of the world." I became extremely confused, because I would constantly hear from the pulpit about gated communities, jets, designer clothes, Bentley automobiles, and other worldly possessions. I found the church to be no different from the world—except at least in the world they were straight up with you as it relates to their intentions. The church is a fake—plus, it is a fake where pastors have found a way to capitalize on poor, emotional people looking to better their lives. I say this because the church takes up multiple offerings every time you enter the doors and attempts to make you feel bad if you can't or don't give.

I ended my six-year relationship with church because I no longer believed in the institution. I'm a real person who has real issues in life. I need to discuss sex, manhood, finances, marriage, and fatherhood in a real environment that is not going to judge me for my thoughts or actions, but aid me in developing a plan of action. I can no longer participate in an institution that is fake in so many respects yet attempts to play the role of a hospital for healing. I do believe I'm a Christian, because I do believe in God, but I don't think that attending a place with four walls can assist me in fulfilling my purpose in life anymore. I need to be in a relationship were there is give and take, not take, take, and take. The church constantly wants your money and time in abundance but rarely gives anything in return; and when it does, it's with limitations.

I'm only human....I'm a man....I'm going to make mistakes. —Rick Ross

Tiffany Maxwell When I left home at seventeen, I left Christianity behind me. And for a little over nine years, I completely forgot about religion of any kind. Well, not completely—I held on to my Christian upbringing for those moments when folks would ask me what religion I was—but in practice and belief, I was no Christian.

In 2000 something piqued my interest in organized religion, and I decided that I wanted to try it again. I decided that in order to grow to my fullest potential, I wanted and needed to be around other like-minded people for support.

It took about six years into a pastor-church relationship for me to realize that I was following another's program. Once again, I came to the realization that I can't blame a pastor and/or the church for my circumstances—only me. And I can't pray to the pastor and/or the church to better my circumstances. My current situation is a direct result of how I have lived in the past. My future will be a direct result of how I live now. Now my "church" is one of self-actualization, individual responsibility, and initiative, the exact things that my family stressed when I was growing up.

Allowing me to believe whatever it is that connects me to God is the path that I will follow. At the end of the day, we are all reaching for the same place. That is my belief. If I focus on my own journey to the divine, I will get there sooner without having to sit in judgment of a preacher's path. My path to living a righteous life and connecting with God may be a completely different journey than the one organized religion is on—and that, my friends, is what makes life so exciting. For the past six years I missed out on living a limitless life due to the pastor-church relationship.

I never know what I am going to get, but if I keep moving, I'll get there and hopefully learn to enjoy the process along the way.

I no longer need a building and its preacher's protocol for life's journey. I have given up on the institution, and I am going straight to God as God guides my meandering journey through life. I am going somewhere.

QUESTIONS TO CONSIDER

1. How many leaders do you have in your church under age forty?

2. What is the percentage of young adults in leadership in your church?

3. Who are the Moseses in your church who may need to retire?

4. How are young adults elevated into leadership?

5. Who are the Joshuas in your church, and how long are they expected to wait before they lead?

6. Who controls the doors to leadership?

7. What mentoring opportunities exist for young adult leaders in your church?

8. How are new ways of leadership being integrated with traditional ways of leadership?

9. Why should the church hold on to the old while embracing the new?

10. What are the tensions in your congregation between the old and the new?

11. What traditions need to change and what traditions need to remain?

NOTES

1. Cora Daniels, *Black Power Inc.: The New Voices of Success* (Hoboken, NJ: John Wiley & Sons, 2004), 119.

2. Bakari Kitwana, *The Hip Hop Generation: Young Blacks and the Crisis in African American Culture* (New York: Basic Civitas Books, 2002), 183.

3. Robert M. Franklin, *Crisis in the Village: Restoring Hope in African American Communities* (Minneapolis: Fortress, 2007), 44.

4. Walter Arthur McCray, *Black Young Adults: How to Reach Them, What to Teach Them*, 2nd ed. (Chicago: Black Light Fellowship, 1992), 1.

APPENDIX A

Invitation Letter
August 28, 2009

Dear _____:

Greetings in the name of our Lord and Savior Jesus Christ.

It is with great excitement and anticipation that we look forward to birthing FAME Young Adult Ministry—GOD-YAM. To this end I want to invite you to an initial meeting to be held on Saturday, September 12, 2009, from 9:30 to 10:30 a.m. at the Allen House. Please bring your Bible.

In His Name,

Rev. Ralph C. Watkins, D.Min., Ph.D.
Minister to Young Adults

cc: Pastor, Rev. Dr. John Hunter

BIRTHING MINISTRY WORKSHEET
FAME Young Adult Ministries

Biblical Foundation
1 Corinthians 9:1-23 and Ephesians 4:11-16
(Evangelism and Edification)

Do you believe this ministry is something
God wants you to do?   ___ yes ___ no
Have you prayed about this ministry?   ___ yes ___ no

Mission Statement: God's Young Adult Ministry at FAME is focused on meeting the needs of young adults. It will offer development, support, edification, and evangelistic programs to meet the specific needs of young adults.

Young adults are those ages 19–39. While the ministry is focused on reaching and ministering to young adults, no one will be excluded from the ministry events. The ministry will be led by a team of gifted and talented young adults who feel called and equipped to minister to this generation.

THINGS THE MINISTRY WILL DO
1. Sponsor a weekly FAME YAM Bible study.
2. Sponsor and plan the FAME & Faith Lecture Series.
3. Sponsor and plan quarterly fellowship events (talks, seminars, workshops, dinners, breakfasts, outings, coffees, etc.).
4. Sponsor and plan the FAME Relationship Dialogue Series: Brothas and Sistas Gonna Work-It-Out.
5. Sponsor and plan a FAME YAM evangelistic effort to include mass media appeals.

NAMES AND PHONE NUMBERS OF PERSONS BIRTHING THIS MINISTRY
[List names and contact information]

YAM INTEREST SURVEY

I am interested in learning and talking about the following topics (please check your top five):

❏ Managing my money   ❏ Career moves

❏ Relationships   ❏ Prayer

❏ Fasting   ❏ Hip-hop

❏ Living a "Christian" life   ❏ Fitness issues

❏ Sex/sexual relationships   ❏ Salvation

❏ Heaven/eternal life   ❏ Dealing with depression

❏ God's purpose for me   ❏ Sin: what is and isn't

❏ Continuing education   ❏ Other: _____

Here is the one question I have about God or about being a Christian:

The one book of the Bible I would like to study is:

_____.

Here is the top need of young adults that isn't being addressed by FAME:

Here is one suggestion for changes and improvements for the young adult ministry at FAME:

Please keep me informed of FAME YAM events.

Name: _____

Address: _____

City: _____ Zip: _____

Phone: _____ Cell phone: _____

E-mail: _____

Check all that apply:

❑ Please add my name to the Young Adult Ministry mailing list.

❑ My e-mail address is listed above. Please send me your monthly e-letter.

❑ I'm interested in volunteering in the Young Adult Ministry Office.

I'm interested in serving on the team for:

    ❑ Sister-to-Sister Ministry

    ❑ Me, Myself, and I Ministry

    ❑ The Meaning of Success

    ❑ Brother-to-Brother Ministry

    ❑ Faith, FAME, and Fitness Sports Ministry

    ❑ FAME & Faith Dialogue Series

Is there anything else we can do for you? Please share:

_____

_____

YAM EVENT SIGN IN

Name: Cell phone: E-mail:

_____

_____

_____

_____

YOUNG ADULT MINISTRY DIRECTORY

Name: _____

Address: _____

Phone: _____ Cell phone: _____

E-mail: _____

Birthday: _____

During the week, I fill my days by:

_____

_____

_____

My favorite things to do for fun are:

_____

_____

_____

My favorite foods are:

_____

_____

I'm really good at:

_____

_____

_____

My favorite things about our church and this ministry are:

_____

_____

_____

How could the church better serve young adults?

_____

_____

_____

SAMPLE MINISTRY SHEET

FAME YAM Ministries

Sister-to-Sister Ministry. This ministry plays a major part in bringing sisters ages 19–39 together. It focuses on dating, relationships, abuse, injury, rape, molestation, violence, and getting along with female friends and family members. The ministry also deals with such topics as sexual orientation and sexuality. Single parenting, teenage pregnancy, abstinence, and birth control are also addressed.

Brother-to-Brother Ministry. This ministry plays a major part in bringing brothers ages 19–39 together. It focuses on dating, relationships, abuse, injury, molestation, violence, and getting along with male friends and family members. It also deals with such topics as sexual orientation and sexuality and staying in one's age range when looking for a partner.

Faith, FAME, and Fitness Sports Ministry. This ministry allows participants of sports to draw closer to God and interact with other members of such sports as basketball, football, tennis, volleyball, running, boxing, fitness, etc. It also caters to health and nutrition, staying in shape, and staying close to God. Special trips will be taken and implemented for all members to go out and enjoy themselves at games, conventions, and outdoor or indoor sporting events.

Me, Myself, and I Ministry. This ministry focuses on the mind, body, and soul of each individual. It deals with the peer pressure we face in society, such as partying, clubbing, smoking, and drinking. It also covers healing (spiritual, emotional, psychological, and mental). This ministry brings in guest speakers on mind, body, and soul and discusses these areas. Along with Bible studies, this ministry has activities to help young adults deal with mind, body, and soul issues. It also touches on self-esteem as well as defining strengths and weaknesses. Moreover, it helps young adults cope with transitions in their lives, such as moving away from home into a new place and dealing with loneliness.

The Meaning of Success. This ministry helps individuals to define who they are on a professional level and define success in their lives. Questions include: How do I recognize success? What does it mean, and what does it look like for me now and in the future? It helps young adults find ways to balance their careers and faith. This ministry sponsors sessions on money management, tithing, and financial planning.

FAME & Faith Dialogue Series. This ministry invites music artists, actors, and speakers to come and talk about their life transitions, how they started in their field, and what effect their faith in God has on their lives. This ministry opens up doors for concerts, movie screenings, conventions, and listening parties.

The Hip-Hop Project. This ministry promotes positive hip-hop and engages in dialogue with the hip-hop community by hosting listening parties and discussion groups and inviting positive artists to the church to perform. This ministry also develops and supports young, upcoming positive hip-hop artists, including those who perform holy hip-hop.

Teams will be formed within all of these ministries, allowing members to be leaders and to use their knowledge and gifts.

///////////////////////

APPENDIX B

The Relationship between the Senior Pastor and the Young Adult Pastor

To Timothy, a true son in the faith: Grace, mercy, and peace from God our Father and Jesus Christ our Lord.
1 TIMOTHY 1:2

The relationship between the senior pastor and the young adult pastor must be founded on trust. As a young adult pastor, you must have the interests of the kingdom at heart while also being committed to the church or ministry you are serving. Your senior pastor is entrusting you with the future of the flock God has made him or her shepherd over. The key to developing a trusting relationship is remembering the order in which you serve. The senior pastor is just that—the *senior* pastor. He or she is to be respected, supported, and submitted to at all costs. If you feel that you can't respect, support, and fully submit to the senior pastor, then you should not serve in that church. If you are already serving and you feel that you can't serve any longer for whatever reason, you should leave quietly and not create a division. If you are leaving with a bad taste in your mouth, leave but keep your mouth shut.

The greatest compliment I ever received came when I moved from First African Methodist Episcopal Church in Los Angeles to serve at a church across town, The City of Refuge. No one from FAME's young adult ministry followed me. The young adult ministry was strong at FAME, and they had a great going-away party for my wife and me. We cried that night, and the relationships that were established continue. But the members of the young adult ministry at FAME stayed put. Why is that a compliment? Because the commitment of the young adult church members to their church is central to the work of their ministry.

Your role as a young adult minister is to build mature disciples of Jesus Christ who are committed to God and to the church as they follow the senior pastor as he or she follows Christ. You should not try to take members, start a church, or incite division. You are there to serve God and the people, not to attract a crowd around yourself for your own self-aggrandizement. People can and will draw close to you as a young adult leader, and they should. These will be close relationships, but they will call for you to remember your position of serving under the senior pastor.

No competition should exist between you and the senior pastor. Don't allow people to play you against your pastor. They will try. The young adult pastor and the youth pastor are traditionally seen as the "hip" pastors, and this may be the case, but don't allow that to be used to cause division. The senior pastor plays the lead role, and the young adult pastor plays a supporting role. Don't ever forget that.

Your support of the senior pastor should be both public and private. You should give no hint of disrespect or disregard for the senior pastor. Any disagreements between the two of you must be held in confidence. Don't allow members of the young adult ministry to get involved in even a perceived disagreement. Causing division in a ministry goes against God's Word.

This leads us to the next point: never do anything that can put you or the ministry in competition or conflict with the senior pastor or the church body as a whole. A violation of this principle can be something as simple as scheduling competing events—this is a "no-no." When we first started the young adult Bible study at FAME, some of the members wanted to schedule it at the same time as the senior pastor's weekly study. This seemed like a good night because people were used to coming then. The only problem was that it put us in competition with the senior pastor's study. Because we didn't want members to have to choose between a young adult event and one led by the senior pastor, we chose another time.

The young adult ministry is not to operate as a church within the church. Young adult ministry is just that—a ministry in the church. As part of their spiritual growth process, young adults should be integrated into the life of the church as members under the shepherding of the senior pastor. You are not the senior pastor, and you should never act like it. Make it clear to those in the ministry by word and deed that the senior pastor is the one they are to follow as he or she follows Christ.

Because young adults are doing new, exciting, and cutting-edge ministry, there will be some tension between the elders of the church and the young adults. Many times the senior pastor may be caught in the middle of a debate. Your role is to side with the pastor. Meet with the pastor and tell him or her what you are hearing, feeling, and thinking, and strategize together how you will respond as a team. Don't be afraid to be honest with your pastor in these types of conversations. Your pastor will grow to trust you more when he or she knows you are honest.

The young adult minister is a model for young adults of what it means to be a mature member of the body of Christ. Ministry members will look to you to see what it means to support a ministry or church while moving it forward. Doing new things in the life of the church that call for change while respecting tradition and the elders may be difficult but necessary. Respect for the past and inclusion of tradition in the new are musts. The young adult minister must call for a both-and approach—not a choice between new and old, but incorporation of the old and the new. When the old and the new are combined with proponents of both respecting each other, something marvelous happens: a coming together of the body of Christ. The young adult minister plays a key role in orchestrating this coming together. As the young adult minister, you must begin with the end in mind, and that goal is to develop mature disciples of Jesus Christ who are no longer tossed to and fro. The result is a ministry that facilitates young adults being integrated as leaders in the life of the church as they grow into mature adults, mature Christians, and leaders in Christ's church.

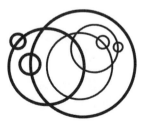